HEALING WOUNDS OF THE PAST

FINDING INNER PEACE AT LAST

by **Don Schmierer**

with **Lela Gilbert**

Promise Publishing Co.  Santa Ana CA 92711

Healing Wounds of the Past

Promise Publishing Co.
Santa Ana CA 92711

Schmierer, Don
With Lela Gilbert
Healing Wounds of the Past
ISBN 0-939497-62-X

This blessed name of Father…must underlie every other name by which He has ever been known.

Has He been called a judge?

Yes, but He is a father judge, one who judges as a loving father would.

Is He a king?

Yes, but He is a king who is at the same time the father of His subjects, and who rules them with a father's tenderness.

Is He a lawgiver?

Yes, but He is a lawgiver who gives laws as a father would, remembering the weakness and ignorance of His helpless children…

Never, never must we think of God in any other way than as "our Father." All other attributes with which we endow Him in our conceptions must be based upon and limited by this one of "our Father."

—Hannah Whitehall Smith (1832-1911)

Acknowledgments

I want to thank Dan and Pat Bibelheimer and Bob Sheffield for sharing some very personal heart-touching stories of their lives. Their walks with God in the difficult seasons of life have encouraged me and I know they will strengthen those who read this book. Thanks for sharing your deepest thoughts. May God's blessings be upon you.

Thank you Ted Yamamori for passing on a personal experience of anger directed toward a race of people which you represent that took place years after a very terrible war for both nations had ended. May your sensitivity to others forever increase.

I want to thank Howard and Roberta Ahmanson for your support and friendship in writing this book. Thank you both from the bottom of our hearts for standing with us.

To my faithful hard-working secretary, Sharron Studinger, a very big thank you. I think you're still re-typing this script in your sleep.

To my loving wife, Diana, many big hugs and kisses for putting up with an "absent-minded" husband as he struggled to write this book.

To Pastor Gus Rauser who, at the young age of 95, is still faithfully living for God and being a pastor to "those older people" through his friendly visits. You're a model of faithfulness to God that I want to emulate, Pastor Rauser. May God strengthen you as you keep up the good work.

Table of Contents

Introduction

"The most important thing that happens between God and the human soul is to love and to be loved." — Kallistos Kataphygiotos

Everyone wants to be loved, to feel loved, to give and receive love. Our human desire for love and for a place of belonging is perhaps life's greatest quest, and it also causes some of life's greatest disappointments. When our longing for love is thwarted or when our loved ones prove themselves to be less than perfect—cruel, critical, mean-spirited, dishonest, disloyal or even abusive—we find ourselves in a world of hurt.

No matter where I go, I encounter hurting people. Perhaps you've had the same experience. In fact, you may be staring into the eyes of a wounded person every time you look in the mirror. If so, and if you've picked up this book hoping to find some answers to your own questions about pain and healing, I'd like to ask you a few questions before we start. You don't have to answer them all right now, but think about them as you read, and we'll come back to them later in the book. For now, just ask yourself…

Who inflicted on you the deepest wound or wounds you've ever experienced?

Do you still feel the pain of that wound (those wounds) today?

Do you ever ask yourself why God allowed some bad things to happen to you? Do you feel anger toward Him?

When you take a long, honest look at yourself, do you see some negative characteristics of the people who hurt you? Are you becoming like them?

Do you believe God is a loving parent, a Father who is proud to have you call Him "Abba" or "Daddy"?

Are you willing to consider becoming "like a little child," and allowing Him to re-parent you, demonstrating His healing power in your life?

Are you ready to forgive and stop beating yourself up?

One of the reasons I want you to think about those questions is because I've had to try to find answers for them many times—to help others as well as to help myself. For the past 40 plus years my wife Diana and I have been actively involved in Christian ministry, which is another way of saying that we've been working with wounded, hurting people for a very long time. We have seen the way pain affects our life choices and how past wounds often limit our ability to function in a productive and fulfilling way.

On parallel track, Ken Canfield, after hearing a speech I gave in Geneva at the World Congress on the Family, pulled me aside and said, "Don, your insights are compelling. Each year I speak to over 10,000 fathers, many of whom are struggling to find healing for their father wound. You must write up your story, ASAP!" Canfield's organization, the National Center for Fathering, does more ongoing training with fathers than any group in the country. I was certainly encouraged by his words because they affirmed my direction, but most importantly, they resonated with my soul.

It has been my experience that inflicted pain and past wounds are different in nature for each person. They may also make a somewhat different impact on males and females. Nonetheless, the path to experiencing inner peace that I want to explore with you is the same, regardless of how the initial wound was inflicted or who caused it. I trust you will be able to apply some of the principles you'll find in the pages that follow to your specific area of wounding—past or present.

I would be negligent if I did not acknowledge that as you read, you will undoubtedly feel the effects of some of your past wounds, and in doing so you could experience some pain that you may not have felt for many years. Furthermore, in an attempt to find common ground with you and not to give the appearance of spiritual piety or a "Here's what you need to do" approach, I beg your indulgence as I share some of my own hurts with you. I have been through the healing process myself, and for the most part, I've obtained my own longed-for inner peace.

Perhaps this is a good place to share some of my personal history of pain and inflicted wounds. I have written more extensively about these experiences in *An Ounce of Prevention* (pgs. 206-209), so I'll summarize here.

Over the years I've worked my way through...

An automobile accident, which took place while I was still in high school, and the injury to my neck still causes severe pain, almost half a century later. My boss had no interest in my injuries and sent me back to the produce fields to work with a neck trauma.

The death of our first baby. After Dean was born, I was praying and thanking God for what seemed to be a very healthy child and rededicating him to the Lord. Even as I was praying, the baby died in a nurse's arms. The phone rang, and I heard the unbelievable words, "Mr. Schmierer, your son is dead—what do you want to do with the body? Also, you'll have to be here early in the morning to let your wife know when she wakes up."

A broken back. When I was 31, a 130-pound bale of hay fell on me, with my pelvis and lower back taking the full blow. Although I was in pain, it was impossible for me to stop working. A month later, the pain had not subsided, and an X-ray indicated that my lower vertebra was cracked, and chipped-off bone fragments were still in the area. The doctor was astonished that I could still walk, and concluded that surgery was too risky. "Grit your teeth and bear it," he advised me.

Chemical poisoning. Over the course of twenty years, the organic fertilizer we used in farming poisoned my system, attacking nerve endings and causing the muscles in my body to spasm continuously. A toxicology specialist in our area checked with other experts worldwide to find out if there was a cure or antidote for my condition. His report back to me was that there is no antidote and that the other doctors could not understand why I was still alive!

Severe migraine headaches. One episode lasted three months. During this time, a friend insisted, "You must be hiding sin in your life to have all these problems."

Financial disaster. When we found ourselves in major debt, and my medical prognosis suggested that within a year I would be unable to work, perhaps even to function, I was nearly suicidal.

Rejection by my father. I've told the story before about my family background. I greatly love and respect my father for demonstrating many godly qualities in his life, but he does have a deficiency in that he is not warm-hearted toward his children, and his inability to express love or validation has been a lifelong source of great heartache for me. When I proudly presented him with my first published book, even though he's an avid book reader he tossed it aside and said, "I'll get to it some day." He changed the subject and to my knowledge has never read the book.

As I drove away in my car, the pain of never being affirmed by my father hit me very hard. At the age of 62 years, I broke down and cried. It really hurt, even though intellectually I had known in advance that he would not give me a compliment. To this day, several years later, my dad has never mentioned the book or asked how it is doing or if I'm doing any other writing. With God's help, I have forgiven my father and moved on with my life; but that doesn't mean it wasn't a very painful encounter.

In the face of all this, I have wrestled with pride, bitterness, confusion, rage and depression. And as years have come and gone, I have learned to release my circumstances to God. "Lord," I prayed during the darkest days of ill health and financial doom, "If allowing me to come to nothing, and if my becoming a burden to my family will bring honor to Your name, You have my permission to do it. Your will be done."

The lessons I learned in the miraculous aftermath of that prayer are the lessons I hope to share with you. God did far more than heal my body—He did a work of grace in my heart, my mind, my personality and in my family. It wasn't an easy process, but my life has been transformed along with the lives of those I love most in the world.

The direction of this book is formed by my own experience with God, and the role He wants to play in all our lives when we experience injustices and long lasting wounds. My desire is that you might have a relationship with the Creator and Sustainer of the universe through His Son Jesus Christ, and that you will grow in His healing grace so that His inner peace may totally permeate your life.

The road ahead will deepen us and will force us to focus on our desire for healing and peace. As author James Houston points out, "The desire that really gives life is to know God. This desire is never satisfied, for it is one that grows with its fulfillment; and our relationship with God changes and leads to a constant deepening of our desires."

Because I want to help you understand and experience healing and inner peace, I will get to the point; my style is going to be straightforward—as we say in the West, "No punches pulled." Most of the examples I use are based on the lives of people I've personally known and talked to over my years of Christian ministry. Their names have been changed, and variations have been made in their stories to protect the wounded from further sorrow.

I will raise some difficult questions about why people hurt people, and why God allows horrible disasters. Through the sections headed "The Challenge," I hope to stimulate your thinking process, but in doing so I may take you out of your comfort zone and make you a little uneasy. My prayer for you, when you've finished reading, is that you will truly experience the peace of God that surpasses all understanding.

For now, let's talk about pain and wounded hearts.

PART I

REAL LIFE IN THE RAW

REAL LIFE IN THE RAW

WOUNDS OF THE FAMILY

> *"I can't explain it, but somehow our identity is inextricably linked to our parents. Our personal fulfillment and personal peace are tied to the kind of relationship we had with them. To regain a relationship with your father and mother, you're going to have to rediscover what they did right. And you'll need to come to grips with the fact that your parents are human beings with needs."*
>
> —Dennis Rainey

The Father Wound

Three young men—Ricardo, Juan and Bobby—were raised in a home where reading of the scriptures and prayer were practiced on a daily basis. The boys' parents were well respected in the community and highly involved in their local church. Not only were the parents involved, but they also took their sons to youth events hoping this would influence their lives in a positive way. All three brothers felt love from their parents, but they never experienced affirmation, a pat on the back for a job well done, acknowledgment of good judgment or applause for demonstrations of their good character. The boys' father was a physically powerful man, who highly valued discipline and frowned on any expressions of emotion. The sons never felt that they measured up to their Dad's "macho" expectations or strict disciplinary standards, no matter how well they performed or what they accomplished.

Ricardo, who has what I would describe as a "sensitive/relational" type of personality, knew that his dad had always disapproved of his career as a professional artist. Despite their differences, however, he decided that he would really put forth an effort to bond with his father by participating in his dad's favorite sport. It was not Ricardo's favorite activity, but he thought maybe a magic spark would ignite and words of approval would suddenly come forth from the father's mouth if he spent some quality time with his now aging dad.

After several days of doing this, nothing seemed to have changed in the father-son relationship. So Ricardo came up with a plan. He sat down with his dad in the kitchen, and said, "You know, you have such a strong character, Dad, and you have always been creative and entrepreneurial, and you've inspired me to choose my own career path—as an artist. I think it's not only a good way for me to use my artistic gifts, but I really love what I do. Dad, I just want to thank you for being such an inspiration and a role model."

Ricardo stopped and looked at his dad hopefully. It was his deepest desire that the older man would respond by offering even the smallest recognition on his choice of a life's profession. At least maybe he'd say, "Ricardo, I don't like your work as an artist, but you've been a good husband and father to your five children."

But that's not the way it happened. Instead, the father stood up and without hesitation, he said, "You're a fool,

Ricardo." Without another word, he turned and walked away, leaving his son sitting there, alone and devastated.

Neil Chethik in *Father Loss* writes after the death of his grandfather,

> *"I had never before heard my father cry. I rose and went to kneel by his side. After a couple of minutes he spoke. 'I am crying not only for my father, but also for me. His death means I'll never hear the words I've always wanted to hear from him: that he was proud of me, proud of the family I'd raised and the life I've lived.' My father then directed his voice toward me and he uttered the words that continue to resound: 'So that you never have to feel this way too' he said, 'I want to tell you now how proud I am of you, of the choices you've made, of the life you've created.' Much of the pain that is inherent in father-son relationships dissolved for me in the calm resonance of that blessing."*

Ricardo has sustained more hard blows in life. One of his sons, who felt called into Christian ministry, died recently after a drunk driver plowed through a stop sign, killing the young man, who left behind a widow with a small child. A hostile client later forced Ricardo into bankruptcy, even though an investigation by the authorities proved him to be above approach.

I talked to Ricardo about life's tough challenges and not being affirmed by his father. He said, "Don, everything I do and everything I am has to do with hearing from my Heavenly Father, 'Well done, My good and faithful servant.' That is what really matters to me above all else that has happened. Also, I will say this, that God has been faithful along the journey of life. He has brought individuals along our pathway that have said to my wife and me, 'God is pleased with you.' For them to say that, not knowing our situation, has been extremely encouraging to us."

Ricardo's brother Juan, who also has a "sensitive/ relational" type of personality, tells a somewhat different story. He has struggled with same-sex attractions since adolescence, and this carefully hidden confusion has caused him tremendous guilt and shame. And although he married and had children, he was never really able to connect with his kids. To make matters worse, he reacted to his father's hard discipline by going the opposite direction with his own family. He did not discipline or set boundaries for his children. It was his hope that being a loving parent would create loving, cooperative kids.

Of course, kids being kids, they were going to try anything they thought they could get away with. And since Juan came from a family situation where there was no dialogue or interaction, but only harshly enforced rules, he was at a loss in dealing with his children's actions until he reached the end of his rope and exploded in rage. Then, while angry, he administered his inherited history of harsh discipline. This sent mixed and confusing messages to his children, resulting in their further alienation from Juan. This style of dealing with problems even carried over into his marriage and chosen profession.

The results of trying to compensate for a wounded childhood still haunt Juan today. He recently told me, "For the first time in my life I really enjoy my family, and it's neat being an 'equal' with them as young adults now." Still, his struggle with same-sex attractions persists, although he now is able to see that he's been seeking the affirmation of an adult male that his father never gave him.

Bobby is the eldest of the brothers in the family, and his chosen profession was to become a drill sergeant in the Army. He has the same "Type A" temperament as his father. He is tough, demanding and always in control of any situation, whether at work or play. I have known Bobby the longest because he was in a Sunday school class I taught some 35 plus years ago. I also spent one-on-one time in discipling him, and both he and his brothers stay in fairly close contact with me.

When I published my booklet, *What's A Father To Do?* I sent him a copy. Would you believe it? At the same time he received my booklet, his 23 year-old son sent him a letter announcing he was joining the gay lifestyle. Both Bobby and his wife were devastated, perplexed and furious about what was happening to their nice Christian family.

Bobby telephoned to tell me about his son's letter and to explain that he had received my booklet. "Don," he told me, "I've read your booklet and I have done everything you said in it. So why is this happening to me? What went wrong?"

Knowing the family quite well, I was able to answer straightforwardly. "Yes, Bobby, from your perspective, you did everything right. But from your son's perspective you did everything wrong." I went on to explain the difference in temperaments between his assertive style and that of his sensitive/relational son, and how the son must have perceived the various actions of his "drill-sergeant" dad. I also told him that there are three things he and his wife must not do to their son: "Don't jump on him, don't damn him or do the things you may feel like doing. Instead, be calm."

One thing about the military, they teach guys like Bobby to follow orders; he willingly followed my very pointed advice.

About a week later, I received an e-mail from Bobby and his wife. They were elated with their son's response to his dad who was clearly in the process of changing. Their son said, "I really did not want the gay lifestyle as much as I totally wanted a real relationship with you, Dad."

A year after that, I talked to Bobby again, and he told me how well his son was doing and thanked me for my help. But now other problems were surfacing. Being the oldest son, Bobby shared some further challenges he was having with his brothers. Since he has been named the executor of his parents' estate, his dad has informed him that he wants to cut his sensitive brother Juan out of the will. He still dislikes him.

With tears in his eyes, Bobby told me, "Don, I told my dad, 'Over my dead body! I will not stand for favoritism like that. And Dad, if you don't like it you can get someone else to handle your affairs.'"

I affirmed Bobby for following the biblical principle of fairness to all. "It must have really hurt you on two fronts," I told him, "confronting your dad and wondering if you did the right thing." In recent years, Bobby has become the true biblical patriarch of the family as the three brothers care for their aging parents.

The Challenge

What were some emotions you felt reading about Ricardo being called a fool by his father? Why do you think Ricardo's father responded the way he did?

A scenario like Juan's has a tendency to end up in same-sex attractions; what can be done to fill the void of no affirmation from the father? Can a father wound like Juan's be healed?

It is said, "You can't teach an old dog new tricks." What did Bobby have to do in order to change his behavior? What did he have to learn?

Does reading these stories bring up any memory of parental conflict in your life? Has it had a positive or negative impact on you?

Can you identify a negative trait from your family history that is plaguing you today?

Hurt People Hurt People. Some forms of abuse are more devastating than what outside observers can imagine. And sadly, the devastation rarely stops with the victim. The ripples from the first event extend far beyond the abused person and his/her family. Sometimes this is called the cycle of abuse, and in various forms it can continue throughout the victim's life. As the saying goes, "Hurt people hurt people."

My own local California paper, the *Lodi Sentinel*, recently reported a study by the Justice Department that "paints pictures of broken lives and gives clues to why more than half a million people ran afoul of local authorities last year.

" 'The tragedy is that people who have been victimized often become victimizers themselves,' said Eric E. Sterling, president of the Washington-based Criminal Justice Policy Foundation."

Author Patricia Love agrees. In her book, *The Emotional Incest Syndrome*, she writes,

> *"It is a distressing but well-documented fact that people tend to pass on the destructive elements of their upbringing. Like dominant genes, dysfunctional behaviors show up in generation after generation, replicating themselves seemingly at will. Children of alcoholics develop drinking or drug problems. Abused children grow up to abuse their own sons and daughters or other children. Children from unstable families wind up with a distressingly high rate of divorce. The tendency is either to duplicate the behaviors we've observed in our families or to run blindly in the opposite direction, creating a whole new set of problems."*

This certainly was "Andy's" story. Andy's father abused his son both physically and emotionally. Andy told me about being beaten when his dad went into one of his rages. His father then tied him up outside in the cold, snowy weather. "I didn't even know my real name until I was around 10 years old," Andy explained. "The name Dad called me was so profane I don't even want to say it out loud."

When I got to know Andy, he had been addicted to both drugs and alcohol, and had been in jail many times. After the ups and downs of working with him for thirteen years, I was grieved to discover that he had become sexually involved with several women outside of his marriage. When we had sufficient evidence, my wife and I confronted him. Our hope was that he would admit to his wrongdoing and seek reconciliation in his marriage. To our disappointment, he denied any involvement. Then he wrote a slanderous letter about me which was sent to our ministry's donor list. When I confronted him about the letter, he flatly told me, "I intend to completely destroy your reputation and take you out of the ministry."

It is hard to describe the pain I felt from this man's betrayal. I had thought of him as a friend, had discipled him, hung in with him through his struggles, and defended him and his past to the Christian community where we served together.

The words written in Psalm 55:12-14 best describe what I was feeling:

> ***"If an enemy were insulting me, I could endure it; if a foe were raising himself against me, I could hide from him. But it is you, a man like myself, my companion, my close friend, with whom I once enjoyed sweet fellowship as we walked with the throng at the house of God."***

Just before Andy and his wife moved out of the area, I approached him again, hoping for forgiveness and reconciliation. After a few brief, superficial greetings, he looked me in the eye and said, "You know, Don, the saddest day of my life was the day I met you. You are to blame for the problems I'm facing in my marriage, and all the rest of this mess I'm in. It's all your doing!"

I politely thanked him, wished him the best, and left the house with a broken heart.

And then there was "Sue." Her father was a psychologist with a thriving practice who helped many of his patients through difficult situations. The dark secret of his life was that he frequently sexually molested all his children—boys and girls alike.

Predictably, once she became an adolescent, Sue became promiscuous in her lifestyle, and her father demanded that she have several abortions resulting from her sexual misadventures. The truth was that he did not want to be embarrassed in the eyes of the community. Later in life when Sue confronted him, the father explained that he had forgiven himself for his past "misdeeds," and that she needed to forgive him, too.

Before his death, all the siblings banded together to confront their father about the way he had misused them. They did so in hopes of enhancing the healing process in their own lives. The mother, however, forbade such a meeting, again fearing that word would get out and his reputation would be tarnished among his clients or the greater community. Unbelievably, he was still practicing therapy.

Sue's story continues to be a sad one. She, Diana and I have spent many hours talking about our heavenly Father and how He can help her. We've tried to explain how her damaged past plays a big role in some of the very poor choices she makes. We have done our best to help her see how, with the Holy Spirit's help, she can overcome her past and live a victorious life. To date, although she goes through periods of progress, not much has changed. She is still promiscuous, dishonest and highly unstable emotionally.

Sue is like Andy in many respects, even though his history involved physical abuse and her abuse was sexual. Sue seems to want to change, and she tearfully expresses her apologies. Being sorry but unrepentant doesn't resolve any of her problems and, like Andy, Sue continues to fall back into her old habits.

The Challenge

In your opinion, what would it take for Andy to receive healing of his father wounds?

What do you think of the possibility that Andy's father could have been a victim of abuse who later became a victimizer? Can the cycle of abuse be stopped? If so, what does it take for this to happen?

In your opinion, when the victimizer does not take ownership for a damagiong act, is healing impossible?

What do you think needs to take place for there to be reconciliation in abusive families?

Can you think of an example of the cycle of abuse in your life or in the life of someone you know?

Wounds from Society

God restrains Himself from constant interference with what takes place on earth, declining to humble every proud man and crush the wicked where they stand, for reasons that continue to perplex their victims. We, like Job (of the Old Testament), assume that God has somehow arranged all events, then draw conclusions that are patently false: "God doesn't love me. God is not fair." Faith offers the option of continuing to trust God even while accepting the limits of our humanity, which means accepting that we cannot answer the "why?" questions.

—Philip Yancey

Falsely Accused

"Fred" had climbed to the top of his chosen profession as a police officer. He was highly successful, and well known in his community. In the course of his police work, he had developed compassion for fatherless boys, and was always involved in mentoring two or three of them. On a camping trip with several youngsters, a boy named Joey accused Fred of sexual molestation.

Joey's mother, when told by her son, immediately informed the community about the incident, and Fred's alleged improprieties were made public by the media. Virtually overnight, Fred was disgraced, fired from his job, and ostracized by his friends. Six months later, just before the trial was to begin, Joey admitted to his mother that the accusation about Fred was a lie.

"Why would you do that?" she asked him.

"I wanted you to pay more attention to me," the boy shrugged.

The same media that had reported the story on the front page of the local paper bypassed this new information. Consequently, Fred's life of public service and his personal reputation were ruined.

Fortunately, Fred and his wife have a solid marriage and they have worked hard to put back together the pieces of their destroyed life. Fred credits his wife's faith in him and her commitment to their marriage, along with God's help, for having the willpower to press on.

Today, Fred has a job that provides for his financial needs and gives him an opportunity to help younger men make wise decisions in their lives. Fred's comment to me was, "Don, I've never enjoyed life so much as now, but what a painful experience to go through!"

Sometimes, as in Fred's case, hurts come in single digits. At other times, the numbers are multiplied again and again.

The Columbine Shootings

The tragic Columbine High School shootings that took place in Colorado stunned the world. Two embittered students shot to death thirteen of their classmates who had never wronged them; in turn, the parents, who were embittered by the horrifying murder of their children, lashed out in lawsuits and accusations at other parents, school authorities, and police. Thankfully, there were exceptions to this pattern, and all the parents didn't seek retribution.

Robert Andrescik wrote in *NewMan* magazine,

> *His daughter was gunned down in cold blood at her school. Now he wants to make sure it doesn't happen to your kids. "We didn't plan a conversation," Rachel Scott's father says warmly, "We just were sitting at the table and by the time we were finished, we were crying; we were hugging each other!" The next morning, Tuesday, April 20, 1999, Rachel was shot three times. A boy sitting on the grass nearby was also shot and badly wounded. But he heard Rachel crying and praying after she had been shot...she tried to*

crawl, and she wasn't able to. She had been shot in the leg, the arm and the side.

Eric Harris walked over to Rachel, lifted up her head by her hair and he said, "Do you still believe in God?" And her answer was, "You know I do!" Then he said, "Then go be with Him," and he shot her through the temple, execution style.

Scott refuses to harbor hatred toward the boys, stating that "unforgiveness only makes you a victim twice"....

Rachel Scott's father was brokenhearted. And he admitted that, had he been in the position to do so, he would have killed the two boys who murdered his daughter and her schoolmates. But he also said that, had the boys lived, he would have visited them in prison. He would have tried to help them learn to take responsibility for their actions. But he would also have tried to tell them about Christ and His forgiveness. "That's what Rachel would have wanted," the father tearfully explained.

Both Fred and Rachel's father, although in very different ways, faced injustice in their lives that brought with it tragic consequences. They had the choice of bitterness or betterment of themselves. With God's help, they chose the latter. It isn't easy, but it is the only wise choice.

Unresolved Past Issues

Tragedy comes in all shapes and sizes. I often have the opportunity to speak at men's conferences. At a recent retreat, I offered two electives aimed at helping men understand gender confusion. Each of these electives drew a small but interested group, and once we'd introduced ourselves, we sat around in a big circle and interacted on the subject. In both instances, several in the group opened up with statements that sounded something like this:

"I was sexually molested when I was a young boy and until today, I have never told another person about it. For whatever reason, I just feel comfortable enough with this group to share this secret. But I wouldn't dare share it in my home church. The fact is, I need help. The pain of what was done to me is affecting my relationship with my wife and family."

A number of men described how they had struggled with pain and rejection because they were somehow "different," and how the "normal" crowd had viewed them as weird. Several shared how they went from being victims to victimizers of young boys. Every one of those who spoke up told about having had a bad relationship with his father and a deep desire, especially as a young man, to be affirmed by a male. This longing for positive male attention was so strong that these men had become attracted to other men which led the way into homosexual behavior. My heart went out to them. All of us who listened felt a great desire to help.

The questions that stayed fixed in my mind were: How can there be so much pain from past wounds and yet there is seemingly no "safe" place for the healing process? What can be done to prevent this kind of pain from being introduced into the lives of today's youth? When will the Christian community wake up to the opportunity to be a safe haven for not only men and women, but also for young boys and girls who are struggling and in pain after cruel abuses, both sexual and physical?

Dr. Elizabeth Moberly, author and expert in homosexual behavior, asks,

> *Is the church truly a community of acceptance and healing, a community of forgiven and forgiving people? In practice, disclosure of homosexuality has all too often led to negative and hostile reactions even if the person in question is a non-practicing homosexual...the church as a whole needs help in reassessing its attitudes.*

Racial Injustice

I was traveling with Dr. Ted Yamamori, President Emeritus of Food for the Hungry when he related an uncomfortable situation resulting from his Japanese heritage in the aftermath of World War II. Here is an excerpt from a letter he later wrote to me about the situation,

> *"While studying at a Christian college in Oregon years ago, I used to guest-preach at the special missions events in the various churches. One Sunday evening, I spoke at a church in rural Montana. The theme was on the church's mission in Japan. The audience was attentive and listened intently to the young Japanese from a Bible college, mainly because his newly acquired English was not so clear and very difficult to understand.*
>
> *"Many expressed delight in my coming to speak to them. It was a good evening of fellowship—until I encountered an elderly woman who hesitantly expressed her real pain in having*

lost her only son in the Pacific during World War II. She said: "I hate the Japanese." Her face had all the signs of agony. "I don't want to hate the Japanese," she continued, "but I can't help myself. After hearing you speak tonight, I realized that the Japanese also suffered from the war."

My response to her, "Half of my house in Nagoya, Japan, was blown up by a bomb dropped from the B29 bomber. The same bomb killed my relatives."

"The war is sin," she said in a hardly audible voice. "I shall continue to pray that the Lord will heal my wounds. I hate the Japanese but not you as a person."

It was a great evening of realization for me early in my ministry that healing comes from knowing the God of peace. Hatred can be removed from everyone's heart only through the reconciliation that will come from above."

Ted's story isn't the same as that of an African-American, but there are many similarities in circumstances and emotional pain. I grew up in central California, so I was quite oblivious to the realities of racial intolerance. My German immigrant family taught me that all people are created equal, and my parents reinforced this in daily practice by hiring a lot of people from a different race than ours to work on our farm. We all worked side-by-side, ate lunch together and sometimes socialized together.

During my high school years, an African-American family came to our community with a desire to minister to high schoolers. To this day, I seriously doubt that my life would be what it is today if I hadn't met them, and if they had not obeyed God's calling on their lives, ministering to us kids. I guess I just loved them, not questioning what and why—hardly comprehending the full ramifications of the fact that blacks were not permitted to stay overnight in our city. They had to sleep in the country, "outside the city gates."

The impact of racial intolerance further came home to me upon returning from an overseas assignment with the Navy when I brought a black friend home with me. He was a hard-working colleague, a gentle man whom we always invited to hit the beach with us. We gave him a nickname and hung out with him both at work and in times of fun and recreation.

A day into his visit with my family, the young man became unusually quiet. So I asked, "What's wrong? Has someone not treated you well? Are you sick?"

His answer hit me like a ton of bricks. "Don," he said, "you and your family have treated me as more than an equal. Yet if I took you with me to the Deep South, I couldn't be seen in a restaurant with you; if we got on a bus, you would sit in the front and I in the back, and I would never be allowed to be with your family socializing together." My heart almost stopped as I began—really for the first time—to feel the pain of racial intolerance and injustice.

And racial, tribal and ethnic injustices aren't limited to the United States. In Africa, I have heard victims tell about the brutalities and slaughter they have witnessed firsthand. It still makes a knot in my stomach as I recall their stories. We hear about ethnic cleansing, tribal wars and religious differences that seem to give humans the right to kill fellow humans. This is not just an African problem, either. It continues in Asia, Eastern Europe, Central and South America and, of course, in the Middle East. Will the cycles of retaliation and uncontrolled anger ever stop?

As I was writing this book, the United States experienced the horror of the terrorist attack on the World Trade Center, the Pentagon and four commercial airliners. Thousands of innocent people lost their lives, which inspired bravery, unification of a nation and the loving sacrifice of many people trying to help in any way they could. But the pain and suffering inflicted by this assault on America is beyond any sane person's imagination. This nation will never be the same. Believers continue to pray for a revival in people's hearts, for God to bring them back to an authentic, obedient faith in God.

THE CHALLENGE

Have you ever been the victim of someone else's prejudices? Are there any prejudices that you can identify in your life?

Have you ever been treated unjustly? How did you respond? How do you feel about that situation now?

Can you think of someone else who has faced injustice? What happened? Who was to blame?

Can bad things happen to good people? When there is no justice given, should God be blamed for this? Do you know a person who is "out-of-sync, a little different"? In light of what we have just discussed, how would you feel about befriending him/her?

How can a person experience the peace of God regardless of what's happening around him/her?

WHERE CAN WE GO WITH THE WOUNDS?

Who's to Blame?

I have been with a mother who was dying with cancer, her heart broken because she was leaving behind a young family to be raised by the father. Not long ago, my wife and I sat with a bereft mother, left to raise her children alone after her husband was killed by a drunk driver. I have seen the devastation of life and property left by what insurance companies call "acts of God," or natural disasters. My heart has ached beyond measure as I have gotten to know the victims among my fellow human beings—shattered souls with human flesh and feelings and dreams just like yours and mine. I could write a volume of books about the wounds and pain I've encountered.

Yes, life is unfair. Life hurts. Life leaves behind the wounded, the broken and the lost. And the question is eventually raised, "So where was God? How could He let this happen?" Sadly, because of anger directed at Him, wounded women and men often refuse to go to the very Source of healing and hope that they so desperately need. Is God, in fact, responsible? I like Phillip Yancey's words in *Reaching for the Invisible God,*

> *When Princess Diana died in an automobile crash, I got a phone call from a television producer. "Can you appear on our show?" he asked. "We want you to explain how God could possibly allow such a terrible accident." Without thinking I replied, "Could it have had something to do with a drunk driver going ninety miles an hour in a narrow tunnel? How exactly, was God involved?"*

Jesus grieved over many things that happened on this planet, a sure sign that God regrets them far more than we do... the Bible supplies no systematic answers to the 'why?' questions, and often avoids them entirely...Divine providence is a mystery that only God understands...no time-bound human living on a rebellious planet, blind to the realities of the unseen world, has the ability to comprehend such answers....

You may be angry with God. You may not even believe in God. And even if you do believe, you may wonder whether He is personally interested in you, and whether He can be trusted.

In the next section, I hope to take a big, wide brush and sketch a portrait of our God based on the way He is described in scripture. This God I'm going to tell you about is not a detached, disinterested energy field or cosmic force. He is not a kindly grandfather who wants us simply to be "happy," and He's not a magic word we can say whenever we want something. You'll also be glad to know that He bears no resemblance to any harsh, disciplinarian father you've known on this earth. In fact, His desire is to do immeasurably more than all you could ask or imagine (Eph 3:20). This is what your Father God said to His people in ancient times, and still says to His people today:

"For I know the plans I have for you," declares the LORD, "plans to prosper you and not to harm you, plans to give you hope and a future. Then you will call upon me and come and pray to me, and I will listen to you. You will seek me and find me when you seek me with all your heart" *(Jeremiah 29:11-13).*

PART II

WHO IS GOD
AND WHAT IS HE LIKE?

WHO IS GOD AND WHAT IS HE LIKE?

The important question is not whether God "exists," it is whether God cares about us and whether we need to care about God's purposes.
—Philip E. Johnson

When most of us face pain of any kind—emotional, physical, mental—eventually our minds turn to God. If we are believers, we try to figure why Father God let the pain happen. We either resign ourselves to presume this is His will, assuming that He had a reason, or we become hurt or angry with Him because He seems to have neglected us. Those who don't know God or who have chosen to believe that He doesn't exist, often use pain as a way of defending their position: "How could a God of love let something like that happen? If there is a God, He would have prevented the pain!"

ASKING TOUGH QUESTIONS

For all of us, when it comes to the subject of God, there are a couple of million-dollar questions. The first one is, "Does God exist?"

The second is based on the first, "Okay, I'm going to assume God exists. But where does God fit into our struggles, our betrayals, our losses, our heartaches, our sicknesses and, ultimately, into our death?"

Perhaps you're still wrestling with the first question.

When I ministered on the University Campus, I was sometimes asked, "Don, can you prove to me that God exists?" My answer was, "Yes, as soon as you will tell me what you will accept as proof."

The questioner would ponder the question for a while and finally get the point. Human beings have finite minds and those minds have limits. Although our finite minds cannot grasp all the complexities of His existence, God has given us His visible and invisible creation so we can know Him (Romans 1:20). If you are struggling with the question of whether God's exists, I suggest that you read Philip Johnson's excellent book, *Defeating Darwinism,* published by InterVarsity Press. This book is based on the truth that God created and designed all things including humankind, and is personally involved in every human life.

The fact is, very few people deny the existence of a "Power greater than ourselves" or a Supreme Being, or some other creative source of cosmic energy. But those impersonal concepts are a far cry from a personal God. When we are hurt, our questions are, "Is God just and fair? Does He care about me?"

Christians believe that the answers to those questions are, "Yes" and, "Yes." In fact, God cares so much that He sent His Son Jesus Christ to live among women and men on earth. Jesus was God-incarnate-as-man. Here are some of the claims Jesus made about himself:

- He said He was the only way to the Father. ***"Jesus told him, 'I am the way, the truth, and the life. No one can come to the Father except through me'"*** (John 14:6).
- He said that accepting Him and His message meant our personal adoption into His Father's family. ***"Yet to all who received him, to those who believed in his***

name, he gave the right to become children of God" (John 1:12).

- He said that He and the Father are One. ***"My sheep listen to my voice; I know them, and they follow me. I give them eternal life, and they shall never perish; no one can snatch them out of my hand. My Father, who has given them to me, is greater than all; no one can snatch them out of my Father's hand. I and the Father are one"*** (John 10:27-30 NLT).

- He said that if we reject Him, He does not reject us, but He gives us the freedom to reject Him. (Jesus speaks), ***"I have come into the world as a light, so that no one who believes in me should stay in darkness. As for the person who hears my words but does not keep them, I do not judge him. For I did not come to judge the world, but to save it. There is a judge for the one who rejects me and does not accept my words; that very word which I spoke will condemn him at the last day"*** (John 12: 46-48).

- He said that He wants to be Lord over every area of our lives. Jesus replied, ***"If you love me you will obey my command"*** (John 14:15). Jesus replied, ***"If anyone loves me he will obey my teaching. My Father will love him, and we will come to him and make our home with him. He who does not love me will not obey my teaching. These words you hear are not my own; they belong to the Father who sent me"*** (John 14:23-24).

A follow-up question about Jesus' saying, ***"No one comes to the Father but by me,"*** is an important one. It goes something like this: "What about people who have never heard the 'good news of the gospel?' Does God automatically reject them without giving them a way of knowing about Him?" My answer is that I don't think so, and here's why:

God has revealed himself, even through nature, so all can know Him:

"For since the creation of the world God's invisible qualities-his eternal power and divine nature-have been clearly seen, being understood from what has been made, so that men are without excuse" (Romans 1:20).

When a person is genuinely seeking Him, God will go to extraordinary measures to bring the good news of the gospel to him/her. God, speaking through the prophet Jeremiah, summed this truth up: *"You will seek me and find me when you seek me with all your heart"* (Jeremiah 29:13).

I know of four such examples of extraordinary measures recorded in the New Testament:

- The Conversion of the Ethiopian Eunuch. This eunuch was searching for biblical answers. ***"Now an angel of the Lord said to Philip, 'Go south to the road – the desert road – that goes down from Jerusalem to Gaza.' So he started out, and on his way he met an Ethiopian eunuch, an important official in charge of all the treasury of Candace, queen of the Ethiopians. This man had gone to Jerusalem to worship"*** (Acts 8:26-27). Philip led the eunuch to Christ, and then left him as miraculously as he had come.

- Cornelius, a Roman army officer, Peter gave the Christian Gospel to Cornelius, a Gentile, through an extraordinary set of circumstances (Acts 10:1-35).

"While Peter was still thinking about the vision, the Spirit said to him, "Simon, three men are looking for you. So get up and go downstairs. Do not hesitate to go with them, for I have sent them" (vs. 19-20). Cornelius found the Lord through this miraculous set of circumstances.

➢ Lydia, the first Convert in Europe. After Paul had attempted to go several other places, he had a vision during the night of a man of Macedonia standing and begging him, ***"Come over to Macedonia and help us"*** (Acts 16:9). ***"One of those listening was a woman named Lydia, a dealer in purple cloth from the city of Thyatira, who was a worshiper of God. The Lord opened her heart to respond to Paul's message. When she and the members of her household were baptized..."*** (Acts 16:14-15).

➢ Paul, the Apostle. ***"About noon as I came near Damascus, suddenly a bright light from heaven flashed around me. I fell to the ground and heard a voice say to me, 'Saul! Saul! Why do you persecute me?' 'What shall I do, Lord?' I asked. 'Get up,' the Lord said, 'and go into Damascus. There you will be told all that you have been assigned to do'"*** (Acts 22:6,7,10). This, of course, was the beginning of Paul's powerful ministry.

These kinds of stories aren't limited to Bible characters; they continue today. I have heard countless reports, many of them from missionaries, about God's extraordinary dispatch of Christians to specific groups or individuals who are seeking to know Him.

I have also heard a lot of questions from university students about the relationship between the Father, Son and

Holy Spirit, such as, "The Trinity confuses me; can you explain it?" My personal understanding of the Triune Godhead is best explained in the following excerpt from a book by Kallistos Ware.

> *"Father, Son and Spirit are one single God, yet each of them is from all eternity a person, a distinct center of conscious selfhood. God the Trinity is thus to be described as 'three persons in one essence.' There is eternally in God true unity, combined with genuinely personal differentiation. There is distinction, but never separation. Father, Son and Spirit – so the saints affirm, following the testimony of Scripture – have only one will and not three, only one energy and not three. None of the three ever acts separately, apart from the other two. They are not three Gods, but one God. The Spirit is God within us, the Son is God with us, and the Father is God above or beyond us. Just as the Son shows us the Father, so it is the Spirit who shows us the Son, making him present to us. It is in and through the Son that the Father is revealed to us:* ***"I am the Way, the Truth and the Life: no one comes to the Father, except through me."***

Maybe I've answered some of your questions. I hope you'll discover some of the realities about God that I've learned to cherish in my own life. God offers more than comfort. He offers power and supernatural intervention into our earthly circumstances.

In fact, when we become truly convinced of who God is and pursue a relationship of love and obedience with Him, we can experience the same dynamics as the New Testament Apostles did. Even though they faced hardship and persecution, they influenced their culture and made a positive impact in their world. You and I can do the same. And, considering the state of our present day culture, the sooner we make an impact the better.

Society's Influence

Much of the pain in today's world comes as the result of tragic cultural influences. These influences include the broken-down family structure, a lack of absolutes, the so-called irrelevance of truth and the moral acceptance of self-gratification as a motivation. The self-absorbed motto, "I can do whatever makes me feel good," lies at the heart of many people's hurtful, destructive behavior.

When society permits it, I can destroy or brutalize others in any way I want to as long as I can sneak past the law. And if my picture of God is twisted or doesn't exist at all, I will be under no higher authority than myself, to do whatever I want, whenever I want.

Before we go on and talk about God's place in our suffering, I want you to think about the following quotes from three excellent writers, who sum up our world's brokenness more eloquently than I could hope to:

- From Floyd McClung: *"Our world is plagued by an epidemic of pain. With divorce rampant and child abuse screaming from the national headlines, it is not surprising that for many people the concept of a Father God evokes responses of anger, resentment and rejection. Because they have not known a kind, caring, earthly father, they have a distorted view of the Heavenly Father's love. In many cases these hurting individuals choose to simply deny or ignore His existence."*

- From Henri Nouwen: *"The best phrase with which to characterize the coming generation is 'the inward generation.' It is the generation which gives absolute priority to the personal and which tends in a remarkable way to withdraw into self. At least three of the characteristics, which the men and women of tomorrow share: inwardness, fatherlessness and convulsiveness."*

- From Gordon Dalbey: *"Christian psychologist Paul Vitz, in a teaching entitled, 'The Psychological Roots of Atheism,' declares that when the father is not present, the child naturally concludes there is no God. The most common false views of God's character–that he is absent, distant, harsh, unapproachable, uncaring, weak–can often be traced to corresponding images of the man's earthly father."*

I believe that without turning to the true God—the God of the Bible—that our world will continue to crumble, and millions of people will be crushed in the process. Even if you don't yet believe in Him, I hope you'll make the decision to seek Him, and eventually to know him. I can promise you that God is closer than you think, and He loves you more than you imagine.

With those ideas in mind, let's take a look at the Bible; the book believers call "God's Word." We'll start at the very beginning to see what we can find out about God's relationship with men and women. In Genesis 2 and 3, we get a look at God's interaction and relationship with Adam and Eve. We will learn that He built and affirmed some very important character traits in them:

Made in His Image

"As a Trinity of love, God desired to share his life with created persons made in his image, who would be capable of responding to him freely and willingly in a relationship of love. Where there is no freedom, there can be no love."

—Kallistos Ware

Then God said, "Let us make people in our image, to be like ourselves. They will be masters over all life—the fish in the sea and the birds in the air, and all the livestock, wild animals, and small animals. So God created people in his own image; God patterned them after himself, male and female he created them" (Genesis 1:26-27 NLT).

God created us, male and female, according to His special design and loving intention. He did this to bring honor and delight to Himself. In His special design, He allowed each of us to have strengths and weaknesses so He could include us in His work. God is not only our Designer and Creator, He is our Father and His love for us is the love of a perfect father for a beloved child.

As we read, we see God placing confidence, opportunity and responsibility in human beings to assist Him in managing His creation in a trustworthy manner. Imagine this—God is trusting man, the crown of His creation, with the care of human life, animals and the environment.

Partnership with Dignity

> ***"So the Lord God formed from the soil every kind of animal and bird. He brought them to Adam to see what he would call them, and Adam chose a name for each one"*** (Genesis 2:19 NLT).

Father God brings Adam into a trusting partnership, and gives him significance and dignity by asking him to name all His animals.

> ***And the Lord God said, "It is not good for the man to be alone. I will make a companion who will help him." "At last!" Adam exclaimed, "She is part of my own flesh and bone! She will be called 'woman' because she was taken out of man"*** (Genesis 2:18, 23 NLT).

Father God identifies in Adam a real felt-need for a companion and immediately meets that need. Imagine how important you would feel about yourself if your earthly father responded to your felt needs before you could even approach him about them. What kind of loyalty and appreciation would that inspire in you?

God's intention for marriage and family began with the first people He made. Family life was part of the perfect world God intended man and woman to live in, before sin entered the picture. Here's what Jesus said about this very essential aspect of life:

> ***"Haven't you read," he replied, "that at the beginning the Creator 'made them male and female,' and said, 'For this reason a man will leave his father and mother and be united to his wife, and the two will become one flesh'? So they are no longer two, but one. Therefore what God***

has joined together, let man not separate" (Matthew 19:4-6).

God created us, male and female, according to His special design and loving intention. God did not separately create homosexuals, although some people have been led to believe that they were "born that way." Because Satan has introduced several myths in our culture about this subject, we need to be sure that we have our facts right. God has set boundaries around all kinds of human activities, including sexual behavior, and He allows us to make choices about those boundaries. However, no matter what boundaries we cross or what choices we make, it's important to understand that God always wants to reconcile with us.

God's Love and Human Free Will

Ask yourself this: What would we be like if God had not given us an opportunity to make choices? Wouldn't that make us into mechanical robots? God completely provided for the first couple with an immense variety of tastes, color and sizes that would continually stimulate them, and keep the zest in their lives. And what did He tell them not to do?

My word picture of God's limitation looks like this: an 8" x 11" sheet of pure white paper with a very small pencil dot on it. Compared with the vastness of the white paper, the dot is very miniscule. That's about the size of God's one demand: He said that the fruit of one tree—one small dot—was not to be eaten. This was His way of giving the first couple a choice in which they could express their love and gratitude towards their Father God through obedience.

The Challenge

In your imagination, try to envision a world where Father God made every person exactly alike. Every man would look identical to every other man; every woman would be a clone of every other woman. There would be no difference in eye color, hair color, size, personality or anything else—how monotonous and boring! Father God made you unique and special. When was the last time you thanked Him for your uniqueness?

If you had been face to face with God, and He had given you the responsibility for His new creation, how would you have felt about yourself? How would you respond to such trust?

How would you feel toward an earthly father who always found a way to meet your needs, even before you asked him?

What gender of people does God bring together to establish a family? Why do you think Jesus affirmed God's two-gender creation?

Does having boundaries in life make you feel more secure or more insecure? Why?

OH NO, HERE COMES TROUBLE!

Now the serpent was more crafty than any of the wild animals the LORD God had made. He said to the woman, "Did God really say, 'You must not eat from any tree in the garden?'" The woman said to the serpent, "We may eat fruit from the trees in the garden, but God did say, 'You must not eat fruit from the tree that is in the middle of the garden, and you must not touch it, or you will die.'" "You will not surely die," the

> ***serpent said to the woman. "For God knows that when you eat of it your eyes will be opened, and you will be like God, knowing good and evil"*** *(Genesis 3: 1-5, NLT).*

The scenarios that took place in the Garden of Eden didn't stop with the first couple. In my estimation, those same scenarios have repeated themselves over and over again throughout human history. In fact, they are still going on. The first scenario is one from Satan, disguised as a serpent that used these tactics:

First, he challenged Eve's intellect and questioned God's specific words, "Is that what God really said?"

Then he cast doubt on—put a spin on—what God had said, presenting only partial truth.

He then indicated that he had superior knowledge—better insight into what God really meant than what the woman had.

Now the hook: he appealed to Eve's emotions—"You know God is really holding out on you! Can't you see that you deserve a better life? You'd better act now or you'll be missing out!"

The second scenario is that Eve either must have been under the tree or at least within sight of it when the serpent approached her. I bring this up because I think we all have a problem with this. In my human nature, I want to see how close I can get to what God has forbidden. Then when we partake or get sucked in, we exclaim, "Why did that happen to me?"

What actually happened in the garden? Was the fall of humanity simply the eating of forbidden fruit? Or was it humankind making a choice not only to disobey Father

God but also to declare their independence from Him? I think the man and woman said, in essence, "Why can't I do things my way and have God's stamp of approval on my actions?" This reminds me of the song made popular by Frank Sinatra, "I did it my way," which has been a motto for all of us at one time or another.

Meanwhile, how did this act of rebellion make God feel? What would be His response to this couple? He had so graciously provided for them, and had shared a daily relationship and dialogue with them. Of course, God is omniscient—He knows everything. But what we read next in Scripture touches my heart. The Bible says that *He went searching for them,* seeking to regain the perfect relationship that He and His created children had experienced together.

You probably know what Adam and Eve did. God found them hiding from Him, and when He questioned them, they started the famous "Blame game," protesting, "It's not my fault!" Because of their disobedience and their declaration of independence, God reluctantly had to ban them from the Garden. They could no longer partake of His free provisions. They could no longer revel in the sheer beauty of His unspoiled creation. Now, instead, they had to face labor, toil and life's harsh realities. In short, it was here that sin and pain entered the world.

Let's summarize Genesis 3:6-24:

- Eve persuaded Adam to cross Father God's boundary and to disobey his instructions.
- Both of them felt shame and tried to hide from Father God.

- Both of them blamed someone or something else for their actions.

- They broke their relationship with Father God—no more walks and conversations in the garden with Him.

- There were long-term consequences of their choices: Adam and Eve had to leave the beautiful garden; life would always be a struggle for them.

- Once they left the Garden, things went from bad to worse. The first family experienced jealousy, envy and cold-blooded murder between siblings. By following God's instructions, Abel's actions brought out jealousy from his brother, Cain. The end result? Abel was killed by his angry brother.

- Meanwhile, Father God had introduced His plan for salvation from sin. He hinted at His plan for reconciliation with mankind when He cursed the serpent. God said, ***"From now on, you and the woman will be enemies, and your offspring and her offspring will be enemies. He will crush your head, and you will strike his heel"*** (Genesis 3:15, NLT). Here God begins to introduce the promise of a coming Redeemer. By using the word "He," God indicates that He is talking about One Person. And since that time, only one descendent of Eve has been born of woman without being born of man – Jesus Christ. Jesus, who fulfilled Genesis 3:15, crushed the head of Satan when He died on the cross for the sins of all humankind and was resurrected by Father God's powerful love.

It is sobering to realize that Father God had this plan in place even before He created the world for mankind. The Apostle Peter wrote, ***"For you know that it was not with perishable things such as silver or gold that you were***

redeemed from the empty way of life handed down to you from your forefathers, but with the precious blood of Christ, a lamb without blemish or defect. He was chosen before the creation of the world, but was revealed in these last times for your sake" (I Peter 1:18-20).

The Apostle John agrees. ***"...the Lamb of God who was killed before the world was made"*** (Revelation 13: 8 NLT).

Father God treated Adam and Eve to the best. He affirmed them. He provided for their every need. He gave them the freedom to make choices. He does the same for us.

The Challenge

God did not intervene and stop Eve from making a choice that had far-reaching consequences. What if he had done so and stopped her? Why doesn't God, as our Father, always intervene in the bad choices we make?

What do you think God was feeling when the couple disobeyed Him?

Do you think Father God really had joy in His relationship with Adam and Eve? Why or why not ?

Could the same kind of separation that shattered this beautiful relationship and caused Adam and Eve to hide from God happen to you today?

Can you recall a choice you made that you would like to erase forever?

If someone paid a high ransom in order to win back a broken relationship with you, how would it make you feel? Can you think of anyone who would do that for you?

SUFFERING SAINTS—
HOW GOD'S PEOPLE FACED PAIN

> *In one word, the whole soul, wrapped up in carnal delights, seeks its happiness on this earth. To counteract this, the Lord by various and severe lessons of misery, teaches His children the vanity of the present life:*
>
> *That they may not promise themselves a life of ease and comfort, He permits them, therefore, to be frequently disturbed and molested by wars or revolutions, by robberies and other injuries.*
>
> *That they may not hanker with too much avidity after passing and uncertain riches, or depend on what they possess, He reduces them to poverty, or at least limits them to mediocrity, sometimes, by exile, sometimes by sterility of the land, sometimes by fire, sometimes by other means.*
>
> *That they may not become too complacent, or delighted in married life, He makes them distressed by the shortcoming of their partners, or humbles them through willful offspring, or afflicts them with the want, or loss of children.*
>
> — John Calvin

Now that we've seen how pain came into the world, we're going to look at several examples of men and women who struggled against various types of tragedy, abuse or family trouble in the Old Testament. Let's take a few minutes to observe the hurtful situations they faced and how trusting in God as their Heavenly Father transformed their lives.

In all of these cases, there was a period of time when, from a human perspective, life was impossible and the future seemed hopeless. I suspect these people asked themselves a question we sometimes ask ourselves today: "Why me? What have I done to deserve this kind of treatment?" In the examples that follow, we can learn some valuable insights about who God is, and how He can transform our circumstances through His involvement in our lives. As we read in Romans 15:4, ***"For everything that was written in the past was written to teach us, so that through endurance and the encouragement of the Scriptures we might have hope."*** We should ask ourselves two questions as we read the stories of God's people in pain:

- How did they respond to their difficulties?
- And what did God do to help them?

Daniel: Injustice vs. Opportunity

Israel was the land of God's chosen people, a nation that received from His hand abundant blessing, prosperity and protection. Unfortunately, the better things got in Israel, the more the people forgot the One who had blessed them. Most of them disrespected God as their Father by disobeying His Laws. They insulted and hurt Him by doing everything conceivable against his good character and nature.

After many years of warning from His spokesmen, the prophets, God withheld His hand of blessing and protection. This happened many times during Old Testament days. In the 6th Century B.C., God allowed many of the people of Israel to be taken into captivity by the king of Babylon.

Among these captives was a young man named Daniel—his story is recorded in the Old Testament book of the same name. Daniel was a nobleman in Israel, and was chosen by Nebuchadnezzar, the King of Babylon, to be one of an elite group of servants in the royal palace. On the one hand, this was a wonderful career move for Daniel—he fared better than most of the other Jews. But on the other hand, he was, like all the Jews, feeling great sorrow about the loss of his homeland. His life had been irreversibly disrupted. Blood had been shed in Israel. Surely he had said final goodbyes to loved ones and friends. And now he found himself in new and challenging circumstances—it was not an ideal situation to be a believer in the true God in the midst of a pagan royal court.

First, he was required to change his name. His original name, "Daniel," reflected his godly heritage; his new name "Belteshazzar" honored a pagan deity, and was offensive to all God-fearing Jews. Naturally, Daniel had to take a crash course in the language of his captors. And all the while, there was ever-increasing pressure on Daniel to compromise his faith in God and to conform to the Babylonian culture.

It couldn't have been an easy time for Daniel. He had reason to be bitter, unhappy and self-pitying. During those painful days, negative emotions could have caused him to make some very bad decisions about his behavior in the king's palace. When we serve God as our Father, we often have to make tough choices. Thankfully, when we make the right ones, they bring about positive results. Here's how making difficult decisions benefited Daniel.

DANIEL'S TOUGH CHOICES AND THE RESULTS (Dan.1-4):

- ➢ Daniel chose not to compromise his godly values.

The result: The King of Babylon appointed Daniel to his staff of advisors.

- ➢ Daniel made a tough choice to stand up for God's honor. He was not afraid to place his life on the line even when all his peers failed and their lives were doomed.

The result: Daniel's uncompromising faith resulted in bringing honor to God.

> ***The King declared, "Truly, your God is the God of gods, the Lord over kings, a revealer of mysteries, for you have been able to reveal this secret"*** (Daniel 2:47 NLT).

- ➢ Daniel's friends were bold and chose not to conform by bowing down to worship a golden image of the king. They didn't obey the king, even after they were threatened by him to be thrown into the fiery furnace. They defied the King's command and were willing to die rather than serve or worship any god except their own God.

The results: God miraculously rescued His servants because they trusted in him. This caused the King of Babylon to give praise to the God of Daniel and his friends. Furthermore, the king promoted them to even higher positions in Babylon. ***"Then King Nebuchadnezzar leaped to his feet in amazement and asked his advisors, 'Weren't there three men that we tied up and threw into the fire?' They replied, 'Certainly, O King.' He said, 'Look! I see four men walking around in the fire, unbound and***

unharmed, and the fourth looks like a son of the gods.'" (Daniel 3:24-25 NLT)

- Daniel's friends chose to leave to God the option of rescuing them or die – either way they placed their trust in their heavenly Father for the outcome.

The result: God used miraculous means to rescue them.

Sometimes when we read stories in the Bible we have a hard time relating to the characters. Maybe it's hard for you to believe, for example, that Father God loves you just as much as He loved Daniel. And do you realize that you are just as capable of making wise decisions as Daniel was? He had been through all kinds of hurt, disappointment and sorrow, but he firmly believed that God was with him in every circumstance he faced. God will be with you, too. He will not only protect and defend you, He will stand with you, walk with you, and even face your greatest challenges with you. You probably won't see Him the way the King of Babylon did, but He has promised *never to leave you or forsake you.*

"Be strong and courageous. Do not be afraid or tremble of them, for the Lord your God goes with you; he will never leave you nor forsake you" (Deuteronomy 31:6). Verse 8 goes on to say, ***"The Lord himself goes before you and he will be with you; he will never leave you nor forsake you. Do not be afraid; do not be discouraged."***

Daniel was in the midst of injustice, and he hadn't done anything to deserve the problems that assailed him. Even in those circumstances, we are able to learn how this man of God responded to pain, struggle and danger. Daniel…

- Did not blame God for his problems
- Did not compromise his absolutes
- Defended God's honor
- Did not conform to ungodly practices
- Gave God the option to rescue him or not

God responded to Daniel in ways that are familiar to us today. He did not take Daniel out of his circumstances, but entered into those circumstances alongside Daniel. He did not prevent Daniel's encounter with the lion's den, but He sent His angel to shut the mouths of the lions.

God allowed Daniel to prove His faithfulness in the king of Babylon's court. Then, seeing that He could rely on Daniel, the King of kings entrusted him with extraordinary prophecies about a far greater kingdom—the Kingdom of heaven. Some of the great cosmic events Daniel foresaw are still in the process of being fulfilled today.

Joseph: Where is God When I Need Him?

Sometimes we try to do what's right and everything seems to go against us anyway. It's times like these when we ask ourselves the question, "Where's God? Why isn't He here when I need him?" The truth is, He's always there. But sometimes, He lets things get very dark before He turns the lights back on. I think we can gain more insights about God's nature by looking at a sketch of Joseph's life. We can read about this Hebrew patriarch in Genesis 39:7-23, and 41:37-40.

One of the first things we learn about Joseph is that he resisted the temptation—even when God seemed far away—to "do what comes naturally."

Joseph was a handsome, well-built man, a dreamer of great dreams and his father's favorite son. His jealous brothers took him captive and sold him into slavery. After arriving in Egypt, he was sold again into the household of a man named Potiphar. As if Joseph didn't have enough problems already, Potiphar's flirtatious wife hit on him, trying to get him to have sex with her. And how did Joseph—who had lots of reasons to, as we say, take care of his needs—respond to her overtures?

Joseph said, "Your husband trusts me and it would be a sin against my Father God." On one occasion, she tried to physically pull Joseph onto a couch with her; Joseph pulled away and rushed for the door. In the heat of passion, Potiphar's wife pursued him and ripped off his shirt.

She was, for good reason, humiliated, rejected and angry. So she falsely accused Joseph of rape, using his shirt as evidence, and had him thrown into jail. For a time, it appeared that Joseph had been a fool to honor his God and his employer.

THE GOD WHO IS THERE

Even in jail, Joseph refused to give in to self-pity, rage or rebellion against God. Instead, he asked Him for wisdom when he was asked to interpret the dreams of some of his fellow inmates. His dream interpretations were so accurate that he was soon asked to interpret dreams for Pharaoh. This is what happened:

> ***"Then Pharaoh said to Joseph, 'Since God has made all this known to you, there is no one so discerning and wise as you. You shall be in charge of my palace, and all my people are to submit to your orders. Only with respect to the***

> ***throne will I be greater than you.' So Pharaoh said to Joseph, 'I hereby put you in charge of the whole land of Egypt.' Then Pharaoh took his signet ring from his finger and put it on Joseph's finger. He dressed him in robes of fine linen and put a gold chain around his neck. He had him ride in a chariot as his second-in-command, and men shouted before him, 'Make way!' Thus he put him in charge of the whole land of Egypt"*** (Genesis 41:39-43).

In the years that followed, Joseph was the second most important man in the land of Egypt. Because he had resisted the temptation to "do what comes naturally," here's what his Heavenly Father did for Joseph:

- ➢ Father God honored Joseph and restored him from abandonment, betrayal and slavery to the #1 position of power and authority under the Pharaoh.
- ➢ Because God had given him divine wisdom, Joseph was able to save his new country from the disaster of a severe famine.
- ➢ Joseph's brothers, who had sold him into slavery, found themselves without food during the famine, which afflicted Israel as well as Egypt. Hearing there was grain stored in Egypt, they went to seek food there, and found themselves face to face with Joseph. When they asked him for food, Joseph forgave them and asked them to bring their families to live with him in Egypt. Thus Joseph was reunited with his grieving father, Jacob, and was able to receive the aged man's blessing.

FAMILY TROUBLES, GODLY RESPONSES

When he was a boy, Joseph had a special, favored relationship with his father who was overly-protective of Joseph and treated him special in many ways. The wrath and jealousy of Joseph's brothers grew and grew, finally peaking when they sold him to a caravan of slave traders. Despite all this, Joseph somehow maintained a positive attitude in dealing with his betrayal and rejection. Even when he had a perfect opportunity to take vengeance on his brothers by refusing to give them food, Joseph responded favorably to them. This resulted in a God-honoring reconciliation with his father and brothers.

> ***"Then Joseph could no longer control himself before all his attendants, and he cried out, 'have everyone leave my presence!' So there was no one with Joseph when he made himself known to his brothers. And he wept so loudly that the Egyptians heard him, and Pharaoh's household heard about it. Joseph said to his brothers, 'I am Joseph! Is my father still living?' But his brothers were not able to answer him because they were terrified at his presence"*** (Genesis 45:1-3).

Did you notice how emotional Joseph was at this turning point in his life? I personally did not know what emotions were until my wife Diana helped me discover them. And I'm not sure if Joseph was able to release, through his tears, all the wounds he'd received all those years. But I do know from this account, and from my personal life, that it is okay to cry, even in a loud outpouring of tears like Joseph's. Through all this, Joseph set a wonderful example for all of us—men in particular—

to follow in dealing with family troubles. He let himself feel his pain and his joy. He was forgiving, gracious, and generous even after all the bad things that had been done to him. To Joseph, that was then and this is now.

Besides exhibiting emotional integrity, how should we respond to life when the worst happens? We can learn a great deal from Joseph. When faced with family betrayal, enslavement, false accusation and unjust imprisonment, Joseph…

- Did not blame God.
- Was faithful to God while living in a pagan culture.
- Did not allow himself to be seduced by an aggressive married woman.
- Forgave his brothers, even when they didn't deserve it.
- Believed that God was able to turn his bad circumstances into blessings.

And how does a loving God respond when one of his children is hurt? We read in Psalm 10:17-18 (NLT), ***Lord, you know the hopes of the helpless. Surely you will listen to their cries and comfort them. You will bring justice to the orphans and the oppressed, so people can no longer terrify them."*** Joseph was a dreamer, but God's response to him was much greater than anything Joseph could have conceived of in his wildest dreams. He literally went from rags to riches at the hand of His Father God, who was, and is,

> ***"…able to do immeasurably more than all we ask or imagine, according to his power that is at work within us"*** (Ephesians 3:20).

Three Special Women

One thing you can't miss when you read the Bible is that God doesn't limit His activity to the lives of men. Throughout Scripture, we see a parade of strong, faithful women who were very important to the fulfillment of God's plan of salvation. Most Christians have heard a lot about Mary, Jesus' mother; the Samaritan woman at the well; and Mary Magdalene, one of the faithful women who first discovered that His tomb was empty.

But I'd like to take a quick look into the lives of a trio of Old Testament women. In each case, their background and family history were against these faithful women. First of all, they were women in a man's world. Second, two of them were foreign—not belonging to the people of Israel. Third, their lives were in shambles before God stepped in.

Thankfully, God does not take gender and nationality into consideration when He chooses the people He will bless. In fact, we read in God's Word a warning against prejudice, ***"...I now realize how true it is that God does not show favoritism but accepts men from every nation who fear him and do what is right..."*** (Acts 10: 34-35).

Despite the cultural challenges they faced, all three of these women chose to move beyond their comfort zone, and to take action steps toward positive change in their lives. As we find recorded in the New Testament book of Matthew, God honored them lavishly.

Rahab (Joshua 2:1-21)

She came from a city condemned by God for its wickedness. She apparently led a promiscuous lifestyle because God's Word describes her as a "harlot" which means she was a prostitute. That's not a good line of work from Father God's viewpoint, but He wasn't looking for a Girl Scout. He knew that Rahab believed in Him as the God of Israel. And He was right—before the battle for Jericho even began, Rahab had risked her life for God's people, hiding Jewish spies and setting herself up for ridicule and rejection by befriending and helping out the people God had chosen. In fact, she must have become one of those chosen people, because she was one of Jesus' great-great-great grandmothers.

Ruth (Ruth 1-4)

She was a Moabite widow, who married a Jewish husband. Ruth's mother-in-law Naomi felt such pain from the death of her husband and two sons that all her hope was drowned in a relentless flood of tears. She found herself alone in the world, and living in a country that wasn't her own. She was devastated. In fact, she changed her name, only allowing people to call her "Mara" which meant "bitter and sad in spirit."

Ruth loved Naomi, and even though it meant she had to live in a foreign country, Ruth chose to be a loyal daughter to this bitter, broken woman. And although Naomi's people had been honored by God, they were strangers to Ruth. Still Ruth loved Naomi, and in the process of expressing her love, she did a lot of things right. Ruth put Naomi's needs ahead of her own, and she honored and obeyed the older woman in every way possible. God rewarded Ruth with a godly loving husband named Boaz, and through Ruth, He rewarded Naomi with a beautiful grandson, Obed. Obed turned out to be King David's great-grandfather—another forebear of Jesus.

Tamar (Genesis 38)

And then there was Tamar (Genesis 38), a woman who was greatly misunderstood and mistreated by her husband's family after his death. Even though her husband's father and relatives denied her rights according to Jewish law, still she chose to remain in the family. She acted courageously and found a way to confront Judah, the family patriarch, for his double standard of righteousness. Ultimately, her courage and commitment to the family resulted in forgiveness and reconciliation. She, too, is named in Jesus' genealogy as recorded by Matthew.

All three women faced potential rejection from family and peers for relying upon Father God's Law, which was given in Deuteronomy 10:17-19: ***"The Lord your God is the God of gods and Lord of lords. He is the great God, mighty and awesome, who shows no partiality and takes no bribes. He defends the cause of the fatherless and the widow, and loves the alien, giving him food and clothing. And you are to love those who are aliens…"***

In spite of their position as outsiders among God's people, these women…

- Did not blame God for the pain they experienced.
- Did not allow the bullying of others to thwart their plans.
- Did not choose resentment or bitterness instead of love.
- Did not fall into self-pity, but instead took action and thus improved their lives.

And how did God respond to them? In every case, as with Daniel and Joseph, these women received far more from God than could possibly be exchanged for the good behavior they offered to Him. They were not only successful in achieving good things for God and blessed by having their names recorded in God's Word, but another, greater legacy of theirs remains today. It was their blood that flowed through the veins of His only begotten Son.

One thing is clear— throughout the Old Testament, Father God continually pursues a relationship with those whose hearts are open toward Him. Two words come to my mind to express the essence of what God asks of us.

- He wants us to *Trust* Him.
- And He wants us to *Obey* Him.

THE CHALLENGE

Can you think of a situation in your life where one of Daniel's good character traits might be important?

Does Joseph's story bring to mind a betrayal or some other damaging incident that happened in your growing-up years that hurt you very much?

Can you recall an injustice or false accusation made against you?

Do you see forgiveness and the refusal to seek revenge as an option or as a necessity?

Have you ever thought that your family history, background or past life was so bad that God could never use you?

Why do you think God honored Rahab, Ruth and Tamar by causing them to be named in the genealogy of His son, Jesus?

FATHER GOD IN THE NEW TESTAMENT

The Old Testament refers to God as Father 11 times, in the New Testament it's 170 times.

—Philip Yancey

*"'**Show us the Father,' Philip asked Jesus, 'that is all we need'** (John 14:8). For a teenager on the threshold of manhood, this translates to, 'Dad, I do appreciate the ways you've taught me right from wrong. But now, I want to see you, the person: What was it like for you growing up? Did you get scared around girls? How do you like your job now? How do you and mom get along?'*

*"And so when in our fear of punishment we had allowed the Law to replace relationship with the Father, God revealed himself personally in Jesus – who answers Philip, **'Whoever has seen me has seen the Father'** (John 14:9)."*

—Gordon Dalbey

Painful experiences with earthly fathers cause problems for a surprising number of people. Some fathers are never available to connect with their children. Others are harsh and critical and unkind. Still others deeply love, but die or otherwise leave the family before their children are ready to let them go. This is such a sensitive subject for so many men and women, that a phrase has been coined to describe it: *The Father Wound.*

One of the marvels of Christianity is that the Creator of the Universe, the King of kings, the Source of all life, has made it possible for us to call Him "Abba," or in modern English, "Daddy." He bridged the gap between sinful humans and His own Presence by sending His Son Jesus into the world—Jesus, human and divine, ***"Begotten not made, of one being with the Father..."***

Jesus came to pay the ultimate price for our souls, to satisfy the economy that says, ***"The wages of sin is death"*** (Romans 6:23). When He died on the cross, the debt of death was paid, once and for all. Because He now lives, through the miracle of the resurrection, we are able to receive eternal life as a free gift from the Father. And we have a right to call Jesus' Father our Father, too. ***"Yet to all who received him, to those who believed in his name, he gave the right to become children of God"*** (John 1:12).

Jesus came to earth to die for our sins, but He also came to reveal the Father to us. He wanted to re-establish the intimacy with His creation that was lost in the Garden of Eden. Philip said, ***"Show us the Father and that will be enough for us."*** **Jesus answered,** ***"Anyone who has seen me has seen the Father..."*** (John 14:8-9). What can we find in Jesus' actions and teachings to display for us a picture of the heart of God? How can we learn from Him what our Heavenly Father is like? I want to share with you some of the teachings of Jesus that really encourage me about the Father's love.

In my view, we have several examples of Jesus displaying the heart of Father God. The first example I want to draw to your attention is found in John 4:4-42. Recorded for us there are a few unique acts where He broke with the tradition of that time in history.

First, Jesus purposely journeyed through the country of Samaria. The Jews hated and considered the Samaritans to be "scum." It was their habit to walk around the area rather than take a shorter route through it.

Jesus violated another taboo not only by talking to, but also by asking a favor of a despised Samaritan, and—worse yet—a Samaritan *woman*. In fact, His interaction with this woman really amounted to an act of honor towards her. I believe she was rather shocked when Jesus didn't insult or judge her even when He knew about her adulterous lifestyle. Instead, He treated her kindly, something that the traditional religious leaders of the time would never have done. This resulted not only in her coming to believe in Jesus as the Messiah, but also in her courageous work as an evangelist. She told her whole town about Jesus, which caused many others there to believe that Jesus was the Son of God.

Second, in the parable of the prodigal son recorded in Luke 15, we again see Jesus going beyond the pious religious exclusivity of His day. In responding to the cold-hearted moral rigidity of the Pharisees and teachers of religious law, one of the stories he used was of a wayward son who left his father's home to spend his inheritance on wild living.

After he hit bottom, ran out of money and had no means of earning an adequate income, the wayward boy chose to admit his foolishness to his father and to return home. Even though the father knew about his son's terrible choices, he was watching the road, longing and waiting for his son's return. No lecture. No silent treatment. He welcomed him with open arms and threw a party for him.

I believe this is a picture of how God, our Heavenly Father, longs for reconciliation with us when we go our foolish ways.

Jesus also addresses an all-too-common pattern in life, something we all wrestle with from time to time. Life is not always perfect, not the so-called bed of roses we dream about. When things go wrong, we sometimes find ourselves wondering where God is, why He doesn't rescue us, and why He allows us to suffer. We saw it happen to Daniel and Joseph, and to the women who weathered their own storms in the Old Testament. But when it happens to us, we are perplexed. I like what Oswald Chambers says about these difficult passages.

As Oswald Chambers points out in his classic devotional book, *My Utmost for His Highest,* Jesus said there are times when God cannot lift the darkness from you, but you should trust Him. At times God will appear like an unkind friend, but He is not like that (Luke 11:5-8); He will appear like an unnatural father, but He is not like that (Luke11:11-13); He will appear like an unjust judge, but He is not like that (Luke 18:1-6).

As we learn about Father God from observing Jesus, we see that He is wise, generous, forgiving, truthful, powerful, grieved by sin, saddened by death, compassionate and entirely focused on speaking the truth about the Kingdom of God. We also notice that He is deeply angered by religious pride and profoundly offended with those who use God's name to usurp His authority for their own selfish purposes.

Buddy Owens, in his book, *The Way of a Worshipper,* creates this poignant portrait of Father God's love.

> *In the year 2000, I attended a Promise Keepers conference in Denver Colorado. On Friday evening, at the downbeat of the opening worship time, I stepped out from the backstage production area to see how the men in the arena were engaging in worship. Seated in the front row*

was a man in his early fifties. His teenage son was seated next to him in a wheel chair. It was dreadfully obvious at first glance that this boy was severely handicapped. I learned later that he had suffered a spinal cord injury playing high school football. The boy was paralyzed from the neck down. He was blind and unable to speak.

When the music started, I witnessed the most remarkable living demonstration of the Father's love that I have ever seen. As 16,000 men began singing "All Hail the Power of Jesus Name," this father turned and faced his son. He slipped his hands beneath the boy's arms, lifted him out of his wheelchair, and held him in a bear hug. There they stood, face-to-face, not more than six inches apart from one another. The father began singing to his son. Slowly, a smile came to the boy's face, like a sunrise breaking through a clouded horizon. The boy was able, with great exertion, to wrap his right arm around his father's neck. And for the next ten minutes, they stood in one another's arms, a proud, loving father singing to his crippled son.

The father's face was full of love and pride for his son, not because of anything the boy could do, but simply because of who the boy was – the father's son – broken, helpless, but beautiful in his father's eyes. As I watched in tearful amazement, I remembered these cherished words from Scripture, ***The Lord your God is with you, he is mighty to save. He will take great delight in you, he will quiet you with his love, he will rejoice over you with singing*** *(Zephaniah 3:17).*

What I saw that night was the Word in flesh, dwelling among us. I saw a father taking great delight in his son, quieting him with his love and rejoicing over him with singing – grace embracing brokenness; joy triumphing over tragedy. In this father's eyes, I saw the love and pride of my heavenly Father. In the son, I saw myself and millions of other broken, helpless people.

The Focus of Jesus' Ministry

As I have examined the life of Jesus as recorded in the New Testament Gospels, I noticed a truth that we sometimes overlook in today's Christian churches and ministries. While training His disciples, Jesus spent the majority of his time conveying to them who He was and the relationship between Himself and God the Father. This was evident in His sermons and parables, and in the miracles.

Although the Twelve had a faint idea that He was the Messiah, the turning point came a week before the Transfiguration. When Jesus asked the disciples, "Who do people say that I am, and for that matter, who do *you* say that I am?" Peter offered a response from the depths of his heart: ***"You are the Christ, the Son of the Living God."***

Several scholars (such as Bill Hull) who have carefully examined the life of Christ point out that once the disciples realized Who He was, Jesus' focus of teaching turned to His earthly mission – the cross, His resurrection and the disciples' evangelistic mission as His witnesses. Scholars differ some as to when this turning point took place, but their consensus (and I agree) places this turning point of emphasis in Jesus' ministry toward the last two months of Jesus' life, around sixty days before He went to the cross.

Using simple math, we can figure that three years of ministry would equal about 1,000 days for Jesus to teach who He is and how He is related to Father God. Then He spent the remaining 60 days focusing on His and the disciples' evangelistic mission to the world. Jesus spent the vast majority of His earthly ministry conveying who He is, which resulted in the disciples following Him even to their death.

Sometimes I think we Christian leaders place more focus on the church's evangelistic mission instead of building a foundation in knowing God. Maybe this is one reason we have reaped church attendees whose moral and ethical standards are no different than those of the world we live in. Perhaps this is also why so many Christians feel so crippled by wounds and other emotional issues—they've never been taught the truth about Father God—how deeply He loves them, how well He knows them, and how able He is to heal them.

We learn about Father God from watching Jesus' actions and listening to His Words. But we can also learn something about God's role as a Father by observing the way He treated His Son. We have recorded for us in the New Testament Gospels how Father God, on three separate occasions, spoke specific words of affirmation to His Son Jesus. These were affirming times in Jesus' ministry because God encouraged His Son so that those around Him heard what He said:

- When John baptized Jesus, God spoke from heaven, saying, ***"This is my Beloved Son, in whom I am well pleased."***

- On the Mount of Transfiguration, God said, ***"This is my Beloved Son, listen to Him."***

- Before the Crucifixion, when Jesus prayed, ***"Father, glorify Thy name,"*** God the Father answered, ***"I have both glorified it (through you), and will glorify it again."***

Jesus' Father thought it was important to publicly and audibly affirm his Son, who was by then in His thirties. This is an important reminder to us that we are adopted children of this same Father—a Father who affirms, encourages, inspires and empowers His children. No matter how our earthly fathers have ignored us, hurt us or have been absent from our lives, we have a Heavenly Father—our "Abba, Father"—Who has bought us with a price, adopted us into His family, rejoices over us (Zephaniah 3:17), has written our names on the palms of His hands, (Isaiah 49:16) and keeps a record of our tears in a book (Psalm 56:8).

God's affirmations of Jesus should remind us, as earthly fathers, to affirm our sons and daughters all their lives, both privately and in public.

Peter—Just Like the Rest of Us

Probably the most touching example of God's love revealed through Jesus is recorded in Mark 14. Here we see Jesus' dealings with strong, self-confident Peter, who declared at the last supper, ***"Even if everyone else deserts you, I never will!"*** Seconds later, he announces that he most certainly won't desert Jesus, ***"Not even if I have to die with you! I will never deny you!"***

Personal strength and courage were some of Peter's best natural qualities. Even so, he ended up denying that he was one of Jesus' friends, cursing when the pressure was on and insisting that he did not even know Jesus. What a crushing blow to Peter's self-image! His actions must have really made him feel completely broken, embarrassed and regretful at having utterly failed in his big chance to display his loyalty to Jesus.

But a few days later, a picture of God's restoring process begins to be revealed. In Mark 16:7, we find Mary Magdalene, Mary the mother of Jesus and Salome walking to Jesus' tomb, only to find it empty. And angel instructs them to tell the disciples—*and Peter*—that Jesus is risen. Jesus didn't, as we say, "shoot the wounded." Instead, he first restored Peter privately (I Corinthians 15:5). He then restored Peter before the others, by allowing him to say, "I love you," three times to publicly contradict his three denials (John 21:15-17).

All too often, the pain we experience in life is made far more excruciating because of regret and remorse—we have only ourselves to blame. We meant well, but we failed to live up to our own expectations. We resolved to do the right thing, then failed to keep our commitment. As Paul wrote, ***"...For I have the desire to do what is good, but I cannot carry it out. For what I do is not the good I want to do; no, the evil I do not want to do-this I keep on doing"*** (Romans 7:18-19).

In the face of our own self-imposed wounds, where can we find hope? When we contemplate the Lord's restoration of Peter, we begin to catch a glimpse of God's love for each of us. Our Father God doesn't hold grudges. He doesn't turn His back on us and walk away, leaving us to writhe in our pain. Instead, He forgives. He reconciles and restores His children, and He does it again and again and again.

Throughout this section, we've looked at men and women who have faced pain and have found their God, their Heavenly Father, their source of strength, courage and, ultimately, blessing. The last example I want to draw your attention to will give you some insight into whether God knows and cares when disaster falls or when injustice is meted out.

Jesus, Standing at Attention

In Acts 7, we read about the first Christian martyr. Stephen was stoned to death after proclaiming God's truth to the same religious authorities who had, not so long before, arrested Jesus and called for His crucifixion. Death by stoning, clearly, is a brutal and bloody mob scene. It must be unimaginably terrifying. Yet the Scriptures state in verses 55 and 56 that while being stoned, Stephen, ***"gazed steadily upward into heaven and saw the glory of God, and he saw Jesus standing in the place of honor at God's right hand. And he told them, 'Look, I see the heavens open and the Son of Man standing in the place of honor at God's right hand.'"***

Jesus is always pictured as *seated* at God's right hand, not *standing*. I want to suggest to you that Jesus was so concerned about Stephen, so in touch with what was happening to one of His faithful servants on earth, that He was standing at attention. With all the persecutions and injustices I see in the world today, we could wonder if Jesus ever sits down.

Interestingly, the sermon Stephen preached, and his subsequent martyrdom made a strong impression on another young man. Paul, who was at that time called Saul, ***"Was one of the official witnesses at the killing of Stephen"*** (Acts 8:1). Then in Acts 22:20 (NLT), as Paul recounts his past life, he states, ***"And when your witness Stephen was killed, I was standing there agreeing. I kept the coats they laid aside as they stoned him."***

My understanding is that Paul was the ring-leader of this horrible crime. Did God abandon him for his evil-doing? No, we know very well that God did for Paul what he did for Peter. He forgave him, restored him and sent him forth into the world as a primary witness to His amazing grace. And ultimately, he allowed both of them to die as martyrs in His name.

The Challenge

Do you think you would have acted differently from Peter in the same situation?

What do you think Jesus felt toward Peter?

What do you think Peter felt toward Jesus?

What do you imagine the other disciples were feeling about Peter?

What did Jesus demonstrate by "not shooting the wounded" Peter?

Do you think Paul would have responded and lived so wholeheartedly for Jesus had there been no Stephen?

Was Stephen's death an ill-timed disaster or something that God used to further His kingdom? Why?

Are you willing to live for Jesus? Are you also willing to die for Him?

If you're like me, you've experienced some deep wounds in your life. And you may have wondered where God was when those wounds were inflicted. I hope I've sketched for you at least a rough portrait of our caring Heavenly Father. He sent His Son to earth not only to live a life reflecting the Father, but also to redeem us from our sins and to give us eternal life with Him.

In John 3:16, Jesus announces, ***"For God so loved the world that He gave His one and only Son, that whoever believes in Him shall not perish but have eternal life."*** Can you agree with what God is saying here and allow Him to be Lord of your life? Why not, in prayer, tell Father God that you are placing your trust in His Son, Jesus. Then thank Him for salvation, and for His free gift of eternal life.

If you have received Jesus as your Lord and Savior, I know that the following words will greatly encourage your heart:

> ***"God's secret plan has now been revealed to us; it is a plan centered on Christ, designed long ago according to his good pleasure. And this is his plan: At the right time he will bring everything together under the authority of Christ – everything in heaven and on earth. Furthermore, because of Christ, we have received an inheritance from God, for he chose us from the beginning, and all things happen just as he decided long ago.***
>
> ***"God's purpose was that we who were first to trust in Christ should praise our glorious God. And now you also have heard the truth, the Good News that God saves you. And when you believed in Christ, he identified you as his own by***

giving you the Holy Spirit, whom he promised long ago. The Spirit is God's guarantee that he will give us everything he promised and that he has purchased us to be his own people. This is just one more reason for us to praise our glorious God" (Ephesians 1:9-14 NLT).

God is not saying here that if we place our trust in a religion, in one particular church or another, in some emotional experience or in a certain charismatic personality, *then* we can become His child. No, it's only when we place our faith in Jesus Christ alone that the Holy Spirit enters our life and confirms that we are God's sons and daughters.

I'm sure you know by now that being a Christian does not exempt us from facing difficulties. Stephen's story alone should have convinced you of that, not to mention all the others we've read about. But now that we have the Holy Spirit indwelling and empowering us, we are able to live a life that brings honor to the Father, no matter what our circumstances may be. In light of that, Paul's prayer for the Colossian Christians is my prayer for you:

"…We ask God to give you a complete understanding of what he wants to do in your lives, and we ask him to make you wise with spiritual wisdom" (Colossians 1:9, NLT).

PART III

HEALING WOUNDS–
FINDING INNER PEACE

HEALING WOUNDS–
FINDING INNER PEACE

"Our world is plagued by an epidemic of pain. With divorce rampant and child abuse screaming from the national headlines, it is not surprising that for many people the concept of a Father God evokes responses of anger, resentment and rejection. Because they have not known a kind, caring, earthly father, they have a distorted view of the Heavenly Father's love. In many cases these hurting individuals choose to simply deny or ignore His existence.

"Jesus Christ is the wounded Healer. He knows how our emotions can be injured. Indeed, He was tempted in every way that we have been tempted. His very birth was questioned, and His mother's reputation was slandered. He was born in poverty. His race was ostracized and His hometown ridiculed. His father died when He was young and in His latter years, Jesus traveled the streets and cities homeless. He was misunderstood in His ministry and abandoned in death. He did all this for you and me. He did it to identify with us in weakness."

—Floyd McClung

Recorded in John's gospel concerning the life of Jesus, we read, ***"And the Word became flesh, and dwelt among us, and we beheld His glory, glory as of the only begotten from the Father, full of grace and truth"*** (John 1:14 NASB).

Father God began His relationship with humans by establishing Himself as a God who demonstrates both grace and truth. Before we go on, let's review some specific ways that Father God reveals His gracious and loving nature to us, based on His relationship with Adam and Eve as recorded in Genesis 1-3.

- Our value as individuals is important to God.
- He created a trusting partnership with us.
- He gives personal identity to us as we fulfill our purpose/work/calling.
- He initiated the relationship process.
- He was sensitive to Adam's needs—*"It is not good that man should be alone"*—and He is sensitive to ours.
- He modeled real love by giving us freedom of choice. We are not robots.
- He allowed us to be dependent, yet to have trust and an unbroken relationship with Him.
- When we declare our independence from God – "I'll do it my way" –we sin, but God comes looking for us, anyway. After necessary consequences, restoration is set in place.
- Before the world was made, Christ gave His life for us (I Peter 1:18-20; Revelation 13:8).

My primary emphasis in the preceding chapter was to show you the "grace" side of God. Jesus, God's Son, is usually framed in the light of compassion, as a good teacher, and as one who "stands up for the little guy."

But Jesus also has some very straightforward things to say. And I have to admit that, at times, I have found myself at odds with His words; my human nature does not always feel like doing what He says to do. His words often hit me hard and I have to make some choices about whether or not to obey Him—or, as He put it, to build my house upon the rock. Will I agree with Him and believe that He knows what's best in my life? Will I decide that He has my best interests in mind when He tells me how I'm to conduct myself? Or will I live my life "my way"?

One of Jesus' most challenging teachings is that we *must* forgive: in order to be forgiven by His Father, we have to forgive those who have wronged us. Jesus couldn't have been more direct when he said, ***"For if you forgive men when they sin against you, your heavenly Father will also forgive you. But if you do not forgive men their sins, your Father will not forgive your sins"***(Matthew 6:14-15).

When we are considering the honor and respect Jesus is due, it is important for us to remember that Jesus Himself experienced the worst injustice possible when Pilate said, ***"I find no fault in him...Crucify him!"*** (John 19:4,6 KJV). Not only did Jesus die unjustly and in unimaginable agony, but He died for us—for you and for me. He not only forgave those who killed him, He made forgiveness available for the rest of us at the same time.

> Ron Julian writes, *"The gospel shows us Christ hanging on a cross and says, among other things, 'this is what you deserve'. When we say we believe the gospel, we are agreeing with God's assessment of our lives. However, this can be a fairly abstract concept at first. Having to forgive someone else takes the abstraction of our own guilt and forces us to deal with it. We find it easy*

to downplay our own sins before God, but we can easily see the guilt of other people's sins against us. Jesus is forcing us to put the two side by side, to agree with Him that the guilt of our sins against God is greater than that of those who have sinned against us. Our willingness to forgive others becomes the sign that our own sins have stopped being abstract to us, that we are willing to look into the eyes of another sinner and see ourselves."

Hebrews 4:15-16 says of Jesus, ***"For we do not have a high priest who is unable to sympathize with our weaknesses, but we have one who has been tempted in every way, just as we are, yet was without sin. Let us then approach the throne of grace with confidence, so that we may receive mercy and find grace to help us in our time of need."***

A key point we learn from Jesus' life is the lesson of forgiveness. But Scripture teaches us that God expects us to do more than forgive. From one end of the Bible to the other, across the centuries, we discover that gratitude and thanksgiving are, like forgiveness, more than options to God's people—they are requirements. And from Paul, who like Jesus also suffered greatly and had to live in what we would consider intolerable conditions, we learn the importance of reaching out and extending help to others, and of comforting others as we have been comforted by Father God. These principles, laid out for us in God's Word, are the foundation stones upon which we are intended to build our lives. They can and will bring healing to the wounds of the past.

LIVING UP TO GOD'S PRINCIPLES

Early in my ministry, I sometimes struggled because I did not have a college degree. I felt this most strongly in the area of counseling, because so many hurting students with problems were coming to Diana and me for help. Then I heard a comment that revolutionized my thinking. It was in a message given by Dr. Henry Brandt, a leading psychologist and teacher of that day. He said that, in counseling, he did not listen to all of his clients' "dirty laundry"—a recital of their dysfunctional families, their past failures and their present unhealthy behavior patterns. Instead, Brandt listened until he heard his clients reveal evidence of some unapplied biblical truth in their lives. He would then stop, point out their oversight and give them an assignment to apply whatever biblical truth they were at odds with. After the client made some progress in that area, Brandt listened further, and repeated the process.

Although I don't have a college degree, I've spent many years living in and learning about God's Word. And I understand exactly what this wise counselor was saying—he was simply focusing on changing people's behavior from disobedience to obedience regarding God's Word. As this process continued, his clients became increasingly responsive to the Holy Spirit's nudging, and started living fruitful lives. This corresponded to what Jesus spoke of in Matthew 7:24-28, when He instructed us to build our houses on rock rather than sand. Jesus describes two different foundations: sand represents the foundation of the foolish person who hears God's words and does not put them into practice; the rock represents the foundation of the wise people who hear Jesus' words and put them to work in their lives.

In James 1:22 (NLT), we are told, ***"And remember, it is a message to obey, not just to listen to. If you don't obey, you are only fooling yourself."*** This makes sense to me as I seek understanding about how to live a Spirit filled and God-honoring life while ministering to other people. I have concluded that God is able to use my walk with Him and my knowledge of His Word to bless others. To this day, I use Brandt's approach when dealing with people's problems. I feel it embodies the approach Jesus used.

Receive Healing, Take Action

One of the things I've noticed in Jesus' ministry is that He always gave the people he healed something to do. Maybe He did so to solidify the miracle or teaching, or to demonstrate that they were truly well. But he often said things like "Stand up!" "Stretch out your hand," "Pick up your bed and walk," "Go and sin no more," and to the people around Lazarus, "Take off his grave clothes and let him go." I think He wants us to respond to Him, too. I believe our healing will be complete and our peace of mind will be restored only when we obey Him. In short, Jesus heals, but we have to take action in response to His healing.

Through the healing process, we will be doing business with the Creator of the Universe, God as our Heavenly Father. I pray He will restore you to the same fellowship with Him today that He had with Adam and Eve before the fall. You and I are not exempt from the fallen world with which Satan raises havoc, but when we put into practice

God's principles, including forgiveness, thankfulness and the comfort of others who are hurting, we can experience inner peace and a life-changing walk with our Heavenly Father.

Agreeing with God About Forgiveness

A year or so ago, I was traveling home from Mongolia and Uzbekistan, hubbing at Frankfurt en route to San Francisco. Hoping to kill a little time by reading, I picked up *USA Today*, August 28, 2001, and my eye caught a subtitle on the front page, "Life: Forgiving Can Feel Good."

The story continued,

> *"Growing evidence is showing there are emotional and physical health benefits derived from the act of forgiveness, psychologist says."*
>
> Inside the paper was the title, *Learning to forgive can benefit the forgiver,* by Marilyn Elias. I quote, *"Forgiving others is a valuable gift to yourself, and even the most grudge-bearing people can learn how to do it, new studies suggest."*
>
> Stanford University psychologist Carl Thoresen continues, *"Mounting evidence shows there are emotional and physical health payoffs from the act of forgiveness."* He made this statement while appearing on a panel at an American Psychological Association meeting. *"But forgiving doesn't mean condoning or deciding to forget offenses, or even necessarily reconciling with offenders"* he went on to say. *"It*

means giving up the right to be aggravated and angry and the desire to strike back."

Can it be that behavioral experts in today's hate-filled world think wounded people should learn to forgive? One thing is certain, when secular psychologists agree with the Bible, there must be something very important going on. Since we're seeking to receive healing from the Lord, let's take a look at exactly what Jesus taught about forgiveness. I'll combine His words with other scripture written to the young New Testament churches.

- ***"So if you are standing before the altar... offering a sacrifice to God...you suddenly remember that someone has something against you...go and be reconciled to that person...then come and offer your sacrifice to God"*** (Matthew 5:23-24).

- ***"If you forgive those who sin against you, your heavenly Father will forgive you. But if you refuse to forgive others, your Father will not forgive your sins"*** (Matthew 6:14-15, NLT).

- ***"Then Peter came to him and asked, 'Lord, how often should I forgive someone who sins against me? Seven times seven?' 'No!' Jesus replied, 'seventy times seven!'"*** (Matthew 18:21-22, NLT).

- ***"But when you are praying, first forgive anyone you are holding a grudge against, so that your Father in heaven will forgive your sins, too"*** (Mark 11:25-26, NLT).

➤ ***"Instead, be kind to each other, tender-hearted, forgiving one another, just as God through Christ has forgiven you"*** (Ephesians 4:32, NLT).

NUGGETS OF TRUTH

"Forgiveness," C.S. Lewis once observed, "is a beautiful word, until you have something to forgive." Lewis is right—forgiveness isn't always easy. My friend Bob Sheffield and I have talked at length about forgiveness. Bob is a tough man, a former professional hockey player, who has been involved in Christian ministry for decades. Although God has used Bob mightily, it is only in recent years that he has begun to really sort out some of the forgiveness issues in his own life. Throughout this section of the book, I will quote Bob, based on excerpts from a conversation he and I recently had.

> **Bob**: My wife and I spent about six years, from 1992 to 1998 involved on a project in Russia, and a number of things happened to me physically. I had a heart attack and had to work myself through that; but probably the thing that best identified my time out there was that I was still dealing with some pretty significant issues that related back to childhood and to the environment that I was raised in.
>
> **Don:** Wow, what happened in those issues?
>
> **Bob:** Well, they came to a head toward the end of our assignment in Russia. I was actually asked to step aside and turn over the ministry leadership sooner than I wanted to. I really had no choice. It was a forced resignation. All the feelings of anger that go with that kind of a situation began to flood into my life, and I realized that even though

the process that was used was quite flawed, the real issues were in my life, my character and some areas that God was speaking on to me.

So the issue was related to me, not to the ministry leaders who had asked me to resign. After that whole process we came home from an overseas trip and I was really burned out and quite angry. A couple of my accountability partners suggested that I immediately resign from the job and start a whole sabbatical period where I could really focus on what was going on. God was very gracious in that I had a couple of divine encounters.

One of them was with a colleague, who said, "Bob, you can focus on how you got into the situation and the people that got you there and be damn angry, or you can focus on what God intends for you to come out with on the other end."

I said, "Well, what do you mean by that?"

He said, "Well, out of 200 case studies that I looked at there are four distinctive things that God seems to do when a person will cooperate with Him."

Of course, I was really interested in what he said the four things were:

Stripping: Like a ship with barnacles. The barnacles aren't wrong; it's just that in the travels of life you acquire some of these things. Wrong or not, they need to be chipped away, so, "look for areas that God wants to strip."

Transformation of character: He said, "Bob, almost always in a situation like this we are looking where God is putting his finger, where He is pointing out an area of transformation of character that we need to resolve."

Possibility of renewed intimacy with Christ.

Renewed Spiritual poverty: He said, "If you cooperate, you can come out at the other end with these things; that's what God offers you."

After taking Bob's thoughts into consideration, some words written by Robert Jeffress seem even more important:

"You know that forgiveness is a biblical concept. Somewhere along the way you also may have been warned about the physical, emotional and spiritual consequences of unforgiveness. Most of all, you are genuinely grateful for a God who was willing to take on human form and die an excruciating death that you might be forgiven of your sins…

"…Continually reliving hurts we've experienced infects not only our life, but also the lives of those around us…Forgiveness provides a way to cut the emotional cord that binds you to your offender…While forgetting an offense may be a result of forgiveness, it is neither the means nor the test of genuine forgiveness.

"The first and often the only person to be healed by forgiveness is the person who does forgiveness…When we genuinely forgive, we set a prisoner free and then discover that the prisoner we set free was us."

Understanding Forgiveness

In my book, *An Ounce of Prevention*, I wrote about forgiveness. Some of the following paragraphs first appeared there, but because of their strategic importance to this matter of healing, I think they bear repeating.

> *Whether our conflict is with God, with others or with our own failures, one of the difficulties many of us have with forgiveness lies in our misunderstanding of what it really means.*
>
> Charles Stanley defines forgiveness as, "*...the act of setting someone free from an obligation to you that is a result of a wrong done against you." That means we are to hand the issue over to God and allow Him to deal with it. In the process, we confront the emotional residue left in our hearts with prayer and through continuously releasing our reactions to God.*
>
> *"That sounds simple enough, but still we fight it. That is because many of our ideas about forgiveness are rooted in false assumptions. The most common of these misconceptions lies in the phrase, "Forgive and forget." In reality, there is no reason to assume that we are likely to forget what has been done to us whether we forgive it or not. Nor should we always forget—it might be dangerous for us to forget. Forgetting could set us up for a repeat performance by an unrepentant perpetrator. Forgetting can also cause us to lose sight of the negative part we may have played in the incident. In short, if we forget, we do not learn from the past."*

Let's return to my friend Bob Sheffield's story:

Not too many years ago, a friend of mine became aware that I was struggling with some things, and he asked me out to dinner. I said, "Fine."

We went out and he immediately disarmed me by asking, "Bob, what's going on in your life?"

I said, "Well, Bruce I don't know, but I'm awfully angry; in fact, I've probably been angry most of my life. "

Now Bruce was very gracious; God used him in a wonderful way. What he said was, "Bob, have you ever gone back to when this started in your life? And particularly any outbreaks or outbursts, where you were really out of control, maybe not outwardly but inwardly you were in a rage? What I'd like you to do is go back as far as you can in your memory and in every one of those situations I want you to stop and think about the people who were involved, think about the situation, confess to God, and reclaim the ground that you gave up to the enemy when you lost it. Because every time you get angry you open up the door to the enemy. "

Well, I went back to the night I was dismissed and there were probably 10 or 15 occasions along the way that God called to mind, and I reclaimed every one of those. It's kind of like a bondage breaker, I suppose. But I was still in this vacuum because I still hadn't touched the core of the issue.

That came a number of months later when a friend was living with us. I had come home and Nancy and this gal were getting dinner ready. We were just chatting and something had gone wrong that day and I said, "I don't know—when I am ever going to get on top of this? " This houseguest was a counselor by training. "Bob, " she said, "let me share a couple of things with you. " She had worked with me for five years in Russia, so she knew me quite well.

She continued, "As I have listened to your story, I picture about a 3-5 year old boy that had to protect himself emotionally in his house because of the violent dysfunctional home where he grew up. That boy is you. You probably checked out emotionally very early in your childhood. Then, because you could get hurt so badly in your home, you determined that when you went out on the street, you would control the environment. And the way you did that was by intimidation, both physical and verbal."

Boy, did she nail that one! As soon as she said it, I told her I had never had anybody unravel and give me the core of the issue. Then I actually could recall instances where I went out into the street or the playground and established control immediately.

For instance, in high school, I remember when I had just started my freshman year. We were having a gym class; I looked around and picked out the biggest guy in the basketball game. The play went the other way and I turned around decked this guy. I absolutely cocked him—knocked him out cold. I never had another confrontation in high school. And I realized that was the way I controlled my environment. It was either physical or verbal intimidation.

Later on, we will see how forgiveness helped Bob deal with his rage and use of intimidation. As he learned, when we forgive, we don't have to forget what happened to us. We do, however, need to lay down the emotional baggage our hurts have caused. With God's help, as we pray for our enemies and seek His best for them, we will be relieved of the rage, bitterness and shame that our past hurts have brought to us. The sooner we can get past the feelings of those things, the better.

Just as forgiveness is not forgetting, neither does forgiveness mean that we trust the person who hurt us. Some people should not be trusted. Trust is earned, not demanded, and we need to develop good judgment about the trustworthiness of friends, family and acquaintances. For example, if a family member has molested your child, has repented and you have forgiven him, that does not mean that you should leave your child alone in his care. That would be absurd. It simply means that you have released him from his past sin. It is foolish, and perhaps even dangerous, to trust an untrustworthy person.

> Chip Dodd has written, *"Discernment is seeking to see clearly the attitudes and behaviors of another for the purpose of making trustworthy decisions in relationships. Discernment grows out of seeking truth, not safety.*

Forgiveness is not trust, nor is it approval of wrong behavior. We don't compromise our moral sense when we forgive – we forgive the sin against us, and in the very process, we acknowledge that it was wrong. Otherwise, there would be nothing to forgive. We don't say, "It's okay." Instead, we say, "It's not okay, but I'm releasing it anyway, and the consequences belong to God."

Some people who are struggling with forgiveness have a particular difficulty with the idea that they are required to reconcile with the person who wronged them. They are hindered by uncomfortable feelings, by mistrust and perhaps even by fear for their lives. In reality, forgiveness is a requirement, while reconciliation may not necessarily be a good idea in all cases.

There are circumstances where we would be foolish to rebuild a relationship with an evil or destructive individual. And there are times when, even though we would seek reconciliation, we cannot achieve it because of the other person's unwillingness. Reconciliation does take two willing persons. Forgiveness neither guarantees nor requires reconciliation.

As Charles Stanley writes:

"Forgiveness does not mean, 'It didn't matter.'

"Forgiveness does not mean, 'I'll get over it in time.'

"Forgiveness does not mean, 'There will be no penalty'"

But you may be facing a different aspect of forgiveness. Right now you may be wondering, after sinning so badly myself, can God ever forgive me?

In my experience, this question is the one asked most frequently by hurting people. And there's another question I always ask in response, whether I know what the person has done wrong or not. I ask, "Is what you've done worse than having sex with another man's wife, and then committing premeditated murder against her husband?" So far no one has claimed to do worse than that.

We have testimony of God's response to those very sins in His dealings with David, the ancient Hebrew king. Interestingly, despite his rather appalling history, God refers to ***"David...a man after My heart, who will do all My will. For David...served the purpose of God in his own generation"*** (Acts 13:22, 36, NASB).

How did God deal with David's sin? God forgave and restored David after he repented, though He allowed him to face consequences for his actions that were very heavy to bear. David was restored and powerfully used in spite of what he had done.

Jesus, in fact, was born through David's family and came through Solomon, Bathsheba's second son, the very woman with whom David had committed adultery. In Matthew 1:6, we read, ***David was the father of Solomon, whose mother had been Uriah's wife....*** And John 7:42 points out, ***Does not the Scripture say that the Christ will come from David's family and from Bethlehem, the town where David lived?***

Of course, to receive God's forgiveness, David had to seek it. Fortunately, we still have the actual text of his prayer for pardon, which is recorded in Psalm 51, (NASB). David begins: ***For I know my transgressions, and my sin is ever before me. Against Thee, Thee only, I have sinned, and done what is evil in Thy sight, so that Thou art justified when Thou dost speak, and blameless when Thou dost judge.***

Like David, like you and like me, my friend Bob Sheffield finally learned his lesson about forgiveness. He concludes his story,

> I obviously grew up in a dysfunctional home where we had all kinds of problems. My mother died an alcoholic. She was 70 when she died, but she died of alcohol related illness. Dad is 90 years old now; he's still alive. He is one of the angriest men I have ever met in my entire life. I love him and hate him at the same time. He's just very hard to be around; he was very hard on people.

And he was emotionally remote when we were kids. He was a hard working man—for 15 years, he worked 12 hour-a-day shifts. Then the union came in and he worked another 12 years on 8-hour shifts where every week his shift would switch. He was tired and out-of-it when he got home. He didn't really know how to be a father. I had to come to a place where I could forgive my dad—not just the fact that he was a remote, distant father, but of all the consequences that he had put on my life. I couldn't even enumerate all those things.

But I know that coming from a dysfunctional home like that, we are terribly starved. Some of the consequences that are passed on to us show up in the way we parent our kids. At least that's the way I parented mine. Some of it was good and some of it was terrible. So we have not only to forgive the person, but also to forgive the effect they've had in our lives.

This thing plagued me all of my life. I fought with this never knowing what the core issue was. Then the final piece of the puzzle in terms of 'real recovery' came in reading Dallas Willard's book, ***Divine Conspiracy***. In this book, he gives an exegesis of the Sermon on the Mount.

The thing that was the "break-through" allowing me to move on was when Dr. Willard talked about ***"Blessed are the poor in spirit."*** He spoke about our spiritual poverty, and that until we come to the place where we are willing to recognize and agree with God that we are spiritually bankrupt, we can't move on.

And then, ***"Blessed are those who mourn."*** You mourn over your own spiritual poverty—not over the spiritual poverty of others, but over your own. In doing so, you come to grips with your own depravity. I think for the first time I really saw my own depravity in all of this. It crushed my spirit. But then Jesus went on and said, ***"The meek will inherit the earth."***

Once you recognize you are bankrupt, you mourn over it and now you are ready to meekly go out and inherit the earth without the anger. When I got that picture in my mind and in my heart it was a transformation.

Well, that's the thing to me that is fun about the Christian life and maybe it keeps me young. I am now 62, and you'd think that I would have a lot of these things figured out. I do have some of them figured out, but the refreshing thing is that God graciously keeps showing me new things that need to be worked on. Lamentations 3: 22 and 23 says, ***"The steadfast love of the Lord never ceases, it's new every morning...and great is His faithfulness."*** I'm testimony to that.

I've see many situations like Bob's in the course of biblical counseling, where people need to peel off the layers of insulation that have grown on top of each other over years of self-protection. The removal of a person's defenses is necessary before either confrontation or forgiveness can be accomplished. At times this may even require professional help. But I want to encourage you to begin taking the necessary steps toward forgiveness. I know scores of people, battling all sorts of addictive behaviors who have experienced growth and deliverance through the forgiveness process. As Tony Campbell writes, "Forgiveness is not a benefit I bestow on someone else. It's a freedom I give to myself."

As Diana and I have worked with men and women who face gender confusion, addictions or struggles with homosexual behavior, we have seen again and again how indispensable forgiveness is to healing. Often wounds that were inflicted in early childhood continue to warp personalities and distort the use of God's perfect design. It is in forgiving those who caused the wounds that true healing and transformation are able to begin.

> In his book, *Growth Into Manhood,* Alan Medinger writes: *Unforgiveness holds countless Christians captive to events of the past. Over and over again, Jesus stressed how we are to forgive as we have been forgiven. Many Christian writers have taken the Lord's command to forgive and have shown how freedom cannot come until we forgive those who in some way hurt us....*
>
> *My experience in ministry tells me that most homosexual men were not abused by their fathers. Most of us had fathers who wanted to be good fathers, but because of something in them, in us, or in the circumstances of our lives when we were growing up, they weren't the fathers that we needed. But we are not in a position to judge them. Who is to say, given how they were dealt with by their own fathers, or given the circumstances of their lives when we were growing up, that they could have done any better? We cannot sit in judgment, we can only forgive.*

Over the course of this book, I have raised the issue of your victimizers' past history, hoping to give you some understanding and identification with those who have hurt us. The hard truth is that if we do not release our victimizers, but continue to demand (albeit retroactively) that they be perfect, our pain will control us and destroy any possibility of our having a healthy life. In short, our abusers will win. Even more sadly, the cycle of abuse will repeat itself through us and will destroy others. My wife and I have observed this pattern for more than 40 years of ministering to people. When will the cycles ever stop?

Stop Beating Yourself Up

We may get past forgiving one another and allowing God to forgive us. but I've noticed that dealing with "life in the raw" and having to face our own inconsistencies and failures, brings up a rather controversial area in forgiveness—that of self-forgiveness. Charles Stanley devotes an entire chapter to this subject, which he calls, "The Challenge of Forgiving Ourselves." He writes,

> *Sometimes the most difficult person to forgive is the one you face in the mirror.... Forgiveness, however, is not complete until you forgive yourself.... If anybody had reason not to forgive himself, it was the apostle Peter. On what must have been the most demanding night of Jesus' life, Peter denied that he knew his Master. Jesus had foretold Peter's behavior, saying,* ***"Before the rooster crows twice, you will deny Me three times."*** *Sure enough, Peter did.* (See Mark 14:66-72.)
>
> *The apostle Paul also was able to forgive himself. He referred to himself as the* ***"chief of all sinners"*** *(I Timothy 1:5, KJV). That may very well have been the case. It is doubtful that anyone persecuted the early Christians with more vehemence and zeal than did Saul (Paul). He breathed* ***"threats and murder"*** *against the disciples of Jesus* (Acts 9:1 NKJV).

But maybe you agree with Chip Dodd's opposing view: "I can only be forgiven by another or by God. I can't crawl up into my lap and say, 'Chip, I'm sorry I did this to me!' I need to ask God and others to forgive me and help me...."

Call it what you will, but what I see in the lives of both the Apostles, Peter and Paul, is that after they repented they did not dwell on their past failures. They didn't keep beating themselves up. To my way of thinking, a person shows disrespect when, after receiving forgiveness either from God or another person, they continue to wallow in the mud of failure and regret. If this is a problem for you, stop beating yourself up and get on with life as God intended you to live it.

The Challenge

1) Do you agree or disagree with these statements?

   - Forgiveness does not mean I will forget—remembering in some situations can be healthy.
   - Forgiveness does not mean I should always in all situations trust the person or persons.
   - Reconciliation is required if forgiveness is genuine.

   Why do you agree or disagree?

2) As you read about the wounds of others, does any situation that you have encountered in the past come to your conscious mind? What incident(s)?

3) If so, what feelings came to the surface: anxiety, inner pain, anger, resentment, thankfulness, inner peace?

4) Do you sometimes enjoy feeling angry? Does it make you feel more powerful?

5) How do you think God wants you to deal with your past hurts?

6) What are you willing to do to get inner peace?

7) Mark the answer that best describes your belief: I believe Jesus is______ interested in me and what I am going through.

___ a little ___ not at all _____totally

8) When I share my pain with Jesus, I feel ...

____guilt _____freedom _____closer to Him.

THANKFULNESS: ANOTHER KEY TO INNER PEACE

"Man is not disturbed by events, but by the view he takes of them."

—Epictetus (ca. A.D. 55-ca. 135).

"Hope is not the conviction that something will turn out well, but the certainty that something makes sense regardless of how it turns out."

—Vaclav Havel

"In everything give thanks, for this is God's will for you in Christ Jesus."

—St. Paul

We have spent a considerable amount of time trying to take a few snapshots of who God is, and of His genuine interest in each of us. We've examined together how God initiated a relationship with the first man and woman, giving them dignity and purpose. Even after they disobeyed God's command not to eat one specific fruit, He still pursued a relationship with them.

Micah, an Old Testament prophet, writes, ***"...the Lord has already told you what is good, and this is what he requires: to do what is right, to love mercy, and to walk humbly with your God"*** (Micah 6:8, NLT).

In another Old Testament passage found in Leviticus 26:12 (quoted in II Corinthians 6:16, NLT) we read, ***"As God said: 'I will live in them and walk among them. I will be their God and they will be my people.'"***

In Colossians 2:16-NAS, Paul instructs us, ***"As you therefore have received Christ Jesus the Lord, so walk in Him."***

And in I John 2:5-6 NLT, we are told, ***"But those who obey God's word really do love him. That is the way to know whether or not we live in him. Those who say they live in God should live their lives as Christ did."*** The very fact that our Father God wants to walk and talk with us is reason enough for a celebration of thanksgiving. What a privilege to have a relationship with the Creator of the universe! What joy that He has promised never to leave us or forsake us. How can we possibly be anything but grateful?

Accepting Life on Its Terms – Bonding with Jesus

Unfortunately, an "attitude of gratitude" is usually the first thing to disappear when the going gets tough. And there are a lot of hard things in life for which we can find no easy answers. We ask "Why?" but are rewarded with silence.

I've been through some of these challenges myself. After one of my accidents the doctor kindly informed me about what probably lay ahead for me. His words still ring in my ears, "Don, your back is so bad, one slip and we'll be pushing you around in a wheelchair for the rest of your life." To say the least, I was not excited about hearing that news or the rest of what he said. "If I operate on your back, you'll have a 50-50 chance of coming out worse than you are now. My advice to you is grit your teeth and learn to bear the pain."

After those words, I felt really depressed and was in the process of crawling into a dark hole of self-pity. I'm not sure how my loving wife handled this, but one thing I do know is that she was praying fervently and relying on the Lord for her strength. Thankfully, a couple of scriptures came to my attention at just the right time, before my emotions hit rock bottom. One was found in Matthew 11:28 NLT, ***"Then Jesus said, 'Come to me, all of you who are weary and carry heavy burdens, and I will give you rest.'"***

I found further words of encouragement in I Peter 5:7 NLT: ***"Give all your worries and cares to God, for He cares about what happens to you."***

What that meant to me was that Jesus cared about my pain and wanted to be with me in it. God was giving me a great opportunity to "bond" with His Son Jesus. Once I realized what He meant, I made a point of thanking Him in prayer every morning for the privilege of giving my pain to Jesus, for sharing in His suffering. After all, He went through the indescribable pain of dying on the cross, and He did it, at least in part, for me. This changed my view of pain. What I had once viewed as a totally negative part of human existence was transformed into something positive—a special identity with Jesus. The pain didn't go away, I just viewed it differently.

This is an important principle, partly because if we want to really know Christ and to experience his power in our lives, we must also participate in the pain He experienced. As Paul writes, ***"I want to know Christ and the power of his resurrection and the fellowship of sharing in his sufferings..."*** (Philippians 3:10). In a similar sense, when we suffer, we are able to enter into the suffering of our Christian brothers and sisters around the world. We can offer up our pain to Christ as an acknowledgement of His suffering and the suffering of His children. Or we can feel sorry for ourselves. The choice is ours.

But as we find the grace to thank God for the struggles, we receive peace in the midst of pain. I think there is a great deal of truth to Vaclev Havel's words, "Healing is best described as the attainment of inner peace." Once we come to peace with our suffering, we are far more able to receive healing. But it only becomes possible to experience God's peace when we express gratitude to Him.

Unfortunately, there are times when we refuse to thank God for our struggles because we resent the fact that He allowed them to happen in the first place. Dr. James Dobson speaks of this candidly in his book, *When God Doesn't Make Sense,*

> *My concern is that many believers apparently feel God owes them smooth sailing or at least a full explanation (and perhaps an apology) for the hardships they encounter. We must never forget that He, after all, is God. He is majestic and holy and sovereign. He is accountable to no one. He is not an errand boy who chases the assignments*

we dole out. He is not a genie who pops out of the bottle to satisfy our whims. He is not our servant —we are His.

And our reason for existence is to glorify and honor Him. Even so, sometimes He performs mighty miracles on our behalf. Sometimes He chooses to explain His action in our lives. Sometimes His presence is as real as if we had encountered Him face-to-face. But at other times when nothing makes sense—when what we are going through is "not fair," when we feel all alone in God's waiting room— He simply says, "Trust Me!"

In Everything....Give Thanks!

Early in our ministry, Diana and I were asked to speak at a youth retreat in the mountains, put on by a church in the area. It was a special time with the college students, and the Lord used our lives to touch many young men and women in their walk with Him. Out of appreciation, the kids gave us a plaque which we proudly placed over the desk in our office. It read, ***"In everything give thanks, for this is God's will for you in Christ Jesus"*** (I Thessalonians 5:18). Whenever the term, "this is God's will for you" appears in scripture, one thing is sure – it's very important to God that we do what He says.

Several weeks after hanging those words over my desk, I received a phone call from a person in our ministry. He began to tell me about the shattered lives of two people we knew and loved, and the longer he talked the worse their situation sounded. I was very disheartened by what I was told. As I hung up the phone, I remember my eyes involuntarily lifting toward the words on the plaque, ***"In everything give thanks…"*** My immediate response was, "God, You've got to be kidding, why would anyone want to give thanks for what I just heard?"

As I allowed the Lord to speak quietly to my heart, I soon learned that the verse says, "In everything"—not "for everything"—give thanks.

In the years since, the Lord has brought to my attention how many times in Scripture the word "thank" appears. I have counted it, in several forms, mentioned 71 times in the New Testament. Here are just a few of examples.

- ***Let your lives overflow with thanksgiving for all He has done*** (Colossians 2:7 NLT).
- ***Let the Holy Spirit fill and control you… you will always give thanks for everything to God the Father in the name of our Lord Jesus Christ*** (Ephesians 5:18,20 NLT).
- ***Don't worry about anything, instead, pray about everything. Tell God what you need, and thank him for all he has done*** (Philippians 4:6 NLT).

Our contemporary society is notoriously ungrateful, unthankful and dissatisfied. I've often wondered why. One reason is that people seem to have a sense of entitlement—we expect everything to fall into our laps when we want it, and whatever our "wants" are, they are also our "rights." Some young adults demand that they start out in life with the material possessions, leisure opportunities and prestige that their parents worked a lifetime to achieve. In my thinking, there's something wrong with that picture.

But a more important point is, why would thankfulness be so important to God?

There are several reasons that occur to me. One is that God wants us to remember that He is the Giver of ***"every good and perfect gift"*** (James 1:17). He makes it very clear throughout His word that His children all too easily forget Him when we have everything we need. Thanksgiving keeps us from failing to remember the One Who has blessed us.

Thankfulness also causes us to focus on the "half-full" glass instead of fixing our attention on the "half-empty" point of view. Life is, at best, a mixed bag of joys and sorrows. By thanking God, we immediately turn our minds toward the good things He has done for us. We become more positive by expressing gratitude.

We learn, too, to thank Him in all things because He has promised, ***"...In all things God works for the good of those who love him, who have been called according to his purpose"*** (Romans 8:28). In hard times, we thank Him in advance for the way He will bring about the best. The Bible talks about a sacrifice of praise, and as with any other sacrifice, it isn't easily offered. Rather than springing forth from a heart overflowing with joy, praise sometimes has to be wrung from a heart that is drowning in tears.

But why is thankfulness so important for our well-being that God keeps emphasizing it? Could it be that by practicing thankfulness we are acknowledging His Fatherhood and Lordship over us? As we saw before, the message of the Old Testament can be summarized in two words that are at the heart of what God desires for us: trust and obey. I personally believe when we are truly living a life of thankfulness, we are developing trust in who God is.

This allows us to view life from God's perspective, and certainly fosters a desire in us to obey Him.

In recent days, the world has heard about the tragic death of Martin Burnham, who died at the hands of Islamic radicals in the Philippines. But few knew of the grateful spirit this man of God maintained under the most intolerable circumstances.

Martin and his wife, Gracia, Christian missionaries, were kidnapped and held captive for a year. Martin was killed by gunfire in a rescue attempt in which Gracia was injured. After returning to the United States following Martin's death, Gracia related a conversation she and her husband had shared after a particularly exhausting day. Martin said, "It's been a very hard year, but it has also been a very good year." They began to thank the Lord for everything they could think of.

"Then," Gracia went on, "we thanked the Lord for every believer that we had ever met, everyone that we could remember." God encouraged the Burnhams' hearts with the thought that every person, couple, family or church they could think of was probably praying for them. Then, Psalm 100:2 came into Martin's mind. It reads, "Serve the Lord with gladness: come before His presence with singing."

Martin said to Gracia, "We might not leave this jungle alive, but at least we can leave this world serving the Lord with gladness." Martin did just that—he was chained to a tree every night for an entire year, and every night, he thanked the guard who chained him up and wished him a good night.

And the last thing the Burnhams did before Martin's death was to pray together. They thanked God for His faithfulness, then laid down for a nap. They were awakened by a firefight between their Abu Sayyaf captors and the Philippine Scout Rangers. With gratitude still on his lips, Martin was caught in the crossfire, and was ushered into the presence of His loving Lord.

The Burnham's story reminds me of Jerry Bridges' words:

> *"To fail to be thankful to God is a most grievous sin. When Paul recounts the tragic moral downfall of mankind in Romans l, he begins with the statement, 'Although they know God, they neither glorified him as God nor gave thanks to him, but their thinking became futile and their foolish hearts were darkened.' To glorify God is to acknowledge the majesty and dignity of His person. To thank God is to acknowledge the bounty of His hand in providing and caring for us. And when mankind in his pride failed to give God the glory and thanks due him, God gave them up to ever-increasing immorality and wickedness. God's judgment came because man failed to honor Him and to thank Him. If failure to give thanks is such a grievous sin, then it behooves us to cultivate a spirit of thankfulness that permeates our entire lives."*

Appreciating What God Has Given You

Sometimes, we don't express gratitude because we are oblivious to the blessings in our lives. We have to change our point of view to see the gifts right in front of our noses.

The old saying, "opposites attract," definitely was true in my relationship with Diana. I'm a type A personality,

"Just like your dad" people told me, and it is my nature to look at life as a series of tasks waiting to get done. Diana is not only more sensitive nature, but to her, everything is relational.

Very early in our marriage, we had a patch of blackberries in our backyard that needed weeding. My plan, which I explained to her, was that we should both start on opposite ends of the garden and work toward the middle until the weeds were gone. To my way of thinking, this was clearly the most efficient way to accomplish the task of weeding the blackberries.

Diana's idea was to work side-by-side with me, weeding down the row, until we reached the end together. Diana was not so concerned with the accomplishment of the task as with the process of doing a task together.

I just wanted to get the job done.

Well, not to bore you with all the challenges we faced in this area, I did painfully begin to learn some very important lessons in life. One lesson was the developing of a relationship with my wife and cultivating friends in the community we live in. Another was to be thankful for this woman who wanted to share her life with me—all things great and small.

And you know, she's got the right idea. When I think of it, Jesus placed a great emphasis on relationships, yet He accomplished all His Father intended for Him to accomplish at the same time. I'm still in the process of learning to model His life. ***"Be humble and gentle. Be patient with each other, making allowance for other's faults because of your love"*** (Ephesians 4:2 NLT). I am constantly grateful for the lessons I've learned from my wife and her heart for people. Thanks to her, I've learned to enjoy relationships almost as much as I enjoy getting a job done!

Sometimes, by the way, it is hard for us men to allow ourselves to be humble and gentle and patient. Because of the role modeling we received in our early years, it seems manly to speak harshly and to take charge of everyone, either through intimidation or forcefulness. I've come to realize that it's not manly at all. I agree with Alan Medinger, who writes,

> *"Jesus was the ultimate man. He never had to prove it, but how clearly He demonstrated it. Gently talking with the woman at the well, protecting the life of the woman caught in adultery, kindly humoring His mother when she insisted that He do something about the wine at the wedding in Cana, taking the little children into His arms, Jesus shone forth with full manhood. Washing the feet of His disciples, He provided the men He had chosen with an example of manly strength put under control for the purpose of serving others."*

A Time for Thanksgiving

Around the same time Diana and I received the plaque, we chaperoned another group of kids on a ski trip. It was planned as an outreach to the college community, intended to bring unchurched young people together in a fun activity with the hope that later on, they would want to know more about Jesus and would choose to attend youth meetings or church.

I wanted to have some sort of spiritual focus that weekend, but we all agreed that a Bible Study or prayer meeting would be too much for those kids who weren't yet believers. "They'll hate it!" one of the other adults told me. "They'll feel like we're shoving religious activity down their throats."

I thought about it for a day or two, and suddenly an idea came to me. What if we just all sat down and shared one thing for which we were thankful? At first, the other adults were skeptical, but finally they agreed. And so we tried it.

Would you believe that it was the high point of the weekend—not just for me, but also for the kids themselves, Christians and non-Christians alike. They talked for weeks about the enthusiasm, the excitement and the spontaneity of that time of thanksgiving. It was uplifting, joyful and a completely positive experience. God has called us to be thankful, and I think I know why—a thankful spirit turns our minds toward heaven, and reminds us that we are not alone.

Here's how Walt Henrichsen puts it, "Thanksgiving becomes a sacrifice when, in the midst of your hurts and disappointments, you affirm His goodness. You delight the heart of God when you don't feel grateful and yet thank Him. People and circumstances cause pain when they impact you in ways contrary to your expectations. Life is full of such hurts...give Him thanks for that pain, this reflects the kind of faith that pleases Him."

THE CHALLENGE

1. Do you find yourself in prayer doing more:

______asking for something

______giving thanks for something?

2. The scriptures state, ***In everything give thanks.*** Is there a circumstance in your life where you have been unable to give thanks?

3. If there is a circumstance where you are unable to give thanks, are you willing to start praying and telling Jesus your feelings about it?

4. Do you have a tendency to focus on negatives rather than positives? Are you willing to change this bad habit by learning to give thanks regularly?

5. Would you consider creating a journal of thanksgiving in which you write at the end of each day all the blessings you have received, the prayers that have been answered, and the reasons you have to say "Thank You!" to God?

Grace, Freely Received and Liberally Given

A Third Key to Inner Peace

"We do not know where we will be two, ten or twenty years from now. What we can know, however, is that man suffers and that a sharing of suffering can make us move forward."

—Henri Nouwen

We've all read the stories in the paper. A mother whose teenage daughter died of anorexia has started an outreach for girls with eating disorders. A mom and dad whose child was kidnapped and murdered have started a support group for other parents with missing children. The surviving victims of a tragedy work together to provide assistance to the families of others who died in the same incident.

Why are some people motivated by their past hurts to reach out? It's simple, really. They've grasped the great truth that using our pain to comfort others gives meaning to our wounds. Sometimes the only way to make sense of a tragedy in our lives is to use it to bless the lives of other people. As Paul wrote,

> ***"Praise be to the God and Father of our Lord Jesus Christ, the Father of compassion and the God of all comfort, who comforts us in all our troubles, so that we can comfort those in any trouble with the comfort we ourselves have received from God. For just as the sufferings of Christ flow over into our lives, so also through Christ our comfort overflows"*** (II Corinthians 1:3-5).

Of course, when we are in the midst of pain and sorrow, we don't always feel like getting involved with others. Healing is a process, and it often takes place in a specific order over a particular period of time. No one should get involved in helping others who hasn't first worked a major part of the way through his or her own pain. Otherwise, there is a tendency to lose ourselves in others' lives, and to use their pain as an anesthetic for our own. Counselors wisely warn against this kind of submersion. Until you have truly forgiven those who have hurt you and are beginning to thank God for your wounds, you probably are not ready to start trying to help other people.

But maybe your pain is beginning to diminish a little. Perhaps the grieving process is nearly over and the tears are only flowing now and then. You're learning how to laugh again. You are feeling occasional ripples of hope. You are beginning to see light twinkling at the end of the tunnel. If so, I suggest that you ask God to begin showing you how you can take your painful past experiences and use them to help others. If you ask Him for wisdom, He has promised give it to you—check out James 1:5.

"But Don," you may be asking, "what do I have to offer? I'm not very eloquent. I can't write books. I will never find the courage to speak publicly. So what are you saying I should do?"

Forgive me for answering a question with more questions, but consider these:

Can you pray?

Can you listen?

Can you deliver food to a needy family?

Can you write letters for someone whose vision is failing?

Can you invite a lonely friend to your home for dinner?

Can you volunteer for a support network or a telephone hot line?

Can you visit a local senior citizens' center?

Can you sing or play a musical instrument or create artwork or write poetry?

Let your imagination go to work. Think about the prayer that follows. How can you bring these wonderful qualities to the people in your circle of influence?

Lord, make me an instrument of your peace,
Where there is hatred, let me sow love;
...where there is injury, pardon;
...where there is doubt, faith;
...where there is despair, hope;
...where there is darkness, light;
...where there is sadness, joy;

O Divine Master, grant that I may not so much seek
...to be consoled as to console;
...to be understood as to understand;
...to be loved as to love.

For it is in giving that we receive;
...it is in pardoning that we are pardoned;
...and it is in dying that we are born to eternal life.

—St. Francis of Assisi

In Search of Christian Community

Protestant Christians in North America seem to take pride in their strong sense of Christian individuality. We thrive on a one-on-one relati onship with God that drives us toward solitary piety and a "Just you and me, God" perspective toward our faith. We like to say, "If I'd been the only sinner on earth, Jesus would have died for me." And we proclaim the fact that no one is responsible for our salvation—no church, no saints, no priests. It's all between

God and us. Sure we go to church to listen to the Word, to worship "where two or three are gathered," and to socialize with other Christians. But our individuality forces us not to rely on others people's faith. After all, only God Himself offers to us the means of grace and the hope of glory.

But there is a major downside to rugged religious individuality. God's Word clearly describes the Church (the body of Christian believers all around the world) as an organism, a single body with many parts (see I Corinthians 12 and Romans 12). Each part of Christ's body—each Christian believer—is uniquely gifted to work together with the rest of the Church. That means your gifts are to be used within the body—they are not meant simply to edify you. Paul wrote, ***Just as each of us has one body with many members, and these members do not all have the same function, so in Christ we who are many form one body, and each member belongs to all the others*** (Romans 12:4-5).

He goes on to say, ***There should be no division in the body, but that its parts should have equal concern for each other. If one part suffers, every part suffers with it*** (I Corinthians 12:24-26).

If the entire body of Christ suffers when you suffer, doesn't it stand to reason that the other parts of the body should comfort you when you're in need of comfort? Consciously and intentionally, shouldn't other believers have the opportunity to share in and get involved in your pain? Sadly, many of us have developed a habit of avoiding others' pain, and of hiding our own because of our pride, and because we are afraid we will be rejected. A true Christian community is one where it is safe to seek comfort and to offer comfort because we all come together with the understanding that we are all, without exception, broken people with wounds that either need healing, are beginning to heal, or have finally been healed.

> Larry Crabb writes, *We need each other, never more than when we are most broken. But brokenness is not a disease, like cancer, that may or may not develop. Brokenness is a condition—one that is always there, inside, beneath the surface, carefully hidden for as long as we can keep a façade in place. We live in brokenness. We just don't always see it, either in ourselves or in others. A central task of community is to create a place that is safe enough for the walls to be torn down, safe enough for each of us to own and reveal our brokenness.... We'd rather be impressively intact than broken. But only broken people share spiritual community.*

Once we have sought healing from our own wounds through forgiveness and thanksgiving, we begin to have the capacity to help others find healing for their wounds. But we can only do this if we are willing to share God's wisdom with them based on our pain, not in a spirit of spiritual superiority, or a demonstration of Bible knowledge, or a "Now that I'm healed, I've got it all together" attitude.

Reaching out to others who are hurting in our church, workplace, school, family or wherever we go, means getting our mind off ourselves and focusing on others. It means empathizing, allowing ourselves to weep with those who weep. This goes against the grain of our modern world, where "Take care of yourself" is a motto we cherish with nearly religious zeal.

Jesus had a somewhat different message. He said in Matthew 10:42, ***And if anyone gives even a cup of cold water to one of these little ones because he is my disciple, I tell you the truth, he will certainly not lose his reward.***

Think about it: Jesus teaches that when we take care of others we are, in fact, taking care of ourselves.

We can, as the saying goes, "turn our scars into stars" by heeding Mary White's words, "Let your grief benefit others. With small steps, begin to reach out to others, for in giving help and care to someone else, your own wounded soul is restored. When we extend ourselves to others, even in small ways, we share another's burden while finding rest for our souls."

What Might Have Been?

Do you remember some of the people I introduced in the first section of the book? All of them were deeply wounded somewhere along the way. And although we can't turn the clock back to spare them their wounds, let's think about how some of the healing principles we've discussed might have made their lives a little less painful.

Suppose, for example, that when the three brothers Ricardo, Juan and Bobby were young boys, their family had been involved in a Christian community where their father's harshness toward his sons was observed by caring, loving people. Other families might have embraced them, and the boys would have benefited from the love of mature believers who cared about them and nurtured their unique personalities. Youth leaders could have encouraged them to grow into men of God by affirming their gender and gently guiding them in their choices. Surely they would have been spared some of the struggles they faced later in life.

Suppose that sometime in his teen years, Andy had found his way into the counsel of a godly friend or family. He might have been taught to forgive, and perhaps eventually even to thank God for the wounds his brutal father inflicted on him. Someone who loved him enough to introduce him to Father God could have steered him away from alcohol and drug use, and from the angry rebellion against society that led to his criminal activity. Chances are he wouldn't have begun his pattern of abusing other people. Instead, he might have been an encouragement to others who had also suffered childhood abuse.

What could have spared Sue? A godly community would have created a climate where it was possible for her to share with a trustworthy adult the truth about her father's molestation. Her mother, too, might have been encouraged to take responsibility for her children and stop enabling her husband's sin. And all of them could have learned the value of forgiveness as a balm for their many wounds.

Fred, the police officer who was lied about by the young boy, was blessed by a godly wife and by Christian friends. He has been able to forgive, to give thanks and to help others. He may not be perfectly whole, but he's come a long way toward healing.

Even today, it's not too late for any of these people to find healing and help from Father God through the hands and hearts of His people. Maybe you think it's too late for you. Perhaps you don't know what to do with your wounds or how to deal with your anger. It's never too late. For now, let's stop talking about other people and think for the next few minutes about you.

In fact, why don't you envision for a moment that you and I are sitting down across the table from each other and enjoying a cup of coffee, tea or just a cool glass of water and talking heart-to-heart. I feel you have gotten to know me through the pages of this book as I have attempted to share my feelings, some of my struggles in life, and my journey towards inner peace.

First of all, may I be so bold as an ambassador of Jesus Christ to say that I believe in you. In my heart I believe that you have a deep desire to experience lasting change in your life. I shared earlier that ***God causes everything to work together for the good of those who love Him."*** **The next verse states, *"For God knew his people in advance, and chose them to become like his Son*** (Romans 8:29 NLT). God has always known you, and has always wanted you to become Christ-like in everything you are and do in life. To accomplish this transformation in your life, God has made available to us the same power that raised Jesus from the dead, and through this power has made it possible for you and me to live a life that pleases Him (Rom. 6:4-11, Phil. 3:10-16). The real issue is this: Will you choose to accept and appropriate that available resurrection power, and make a daily effort to reflect the character of Jesus as revealed in the Gospels?

That brings us back to the beginning. Once again, let's reflect on some of the key questions that I first asked you to consider when you started reading. And the real issue is, of course, what kind of action are you going to take once you've answered them. Please reconsider the following, and this time take the time to find the answers within yourself…

- Who inflicted the deepest wound or wounds you've ever experienced?

- Do you still feel the pain of that wound (those wounds) today?

- Do you ever ask yourself why God allowed some bad things to happen to you? Do you feel anger toward Him?

- When you take a long, honest look at yourself, do you see some negative characteristics of the person who wounded you? Are you becoming like them?

- Do you believe God is a loving parent, a Father who is proud to have you call Him "Abba" or "Daddy?"

- Are you willing to consider becoming "like a little child," and allowing Him to re-parent you, demonstrating His healing power in your life?

- Are you ready to forgive and stop beating yourself up?

Now that you've reviewed those questions, please allow me to ask you a few more…

- Do you often feel anger toward others? Do you have a need to control, a desire for vengeance or a habit of intimidating others to compensate for your terrifying feelings of powerlessness?

- If you're honest, can you see that people close to you are suffering in some way as a result of your behavior?

- Are you willing to admit that you have hurt others because of your own wound? Has your bad behavior been a defense meant to protect the wound? Do you wound others when you rage about it, hide it or disguise it?

- Are you willing to release the anger you feel, to give up the surge of power the anger gives you, and to hand all vengeance over to God?
- Are you ready to experience powerlessness so that God can be strong in your weakness?
- Are you willing to forgive everyone who has hurt you?
- After forgiving a person and if the hurt feeling resurfaces, are you willing to use that as a reminder from Jesus to pray a blessing from Him on that person? (Luke 6:27-28).
- Are you willing to say "Thank You" for everything that has ever happened to you? Can you believe God is able to work all things together for good—even the worst things that have happened to you?
- Once you begin to feel God's healing power, will you consider reaching out to others in order to bring healing to the body of Christ, and to share the comfort God has extended to you?

A special Friend of mine, whom I call my Heavenly Father, is waiting to occupy my chair and is anxious to hear what you have to say. On the next page you will find my suggestion for a place to begin your conversation with Father God. Read on!

The Challenge

Now that you have a quiet place where you can be alone, may I suggest a prayer to say aloud to Father God? You may want to include a pastor, a trustworthy friend or your spouse to pray with you:

Father God, I thank You for being a Father to the fatherless, a Physician to the wounded, a Counselor to the confused, and a Friend to the friendless.

Thank You for seeing my pain, and for wanting to make me whole.

Thank You for Your patience with me when I've acted like a victim instead of choosing to be, with Your help, victorious over my past.

Thank You for sending Your Son to die for me so I can live an abundant life.

Lord, please forgive the times I've wounded others because of my own brokenness. Please forgive my sins as I forgive others their sins against me.

Lord, Thank You for the bad things as well as the good, especially for (please name the wound).

Lord, as I allow You to heal me, please give me the opportunity and the courage to reach out healing hands to others.

Make me an instrument of Your peace, Father God.

In Jesus' name,

Amen

PART IV

A STRUGGLER'S JOURNAL

A STRUGGLER'S JOURNAL

In recent months, I have run across something very rare—a man writing an ongoing journal of his thoughts and feelings as he struggles with the news of his wife's cancer and the ensuing faith journey. Dan and Pat Bibelheimer are friends, as well as cousins to my wife Diana. Dan is an M.D.—a General Practitioner—in Grass Valley, California. He sends e-mail reports to their friends and loved ones, keeping us all informed about their progress and prayer requests.

Dan and Pat have looked death in the face, and have found the strength to say, along with Job (42:5), ***I have heard about you before, but now I have seen you with my own eyes.*** Some of the rich nuggets their hearts open for us to see include…

- What marriage commitment is all about.
- The value of having supportive friends and family.
- Dealing with baffling emotional swings.
- Dependence on God and prayer.
- Living each day to its fullest.
- Keeping dreams alive.
- Being thankful for little things.
- Sensitivity to others' suffering.
- Maintaining meaningful and hopeful conversations.
- Balancing negative and positive thoughts.

Dan explained about the journals, *While I want to stay positive and optimistic, in the dark of night, deep in my heart, I fear this may just be the beginning of a long, hard journey. Fortunately, we have made a good investment over the years in friendships and you mean a lot to us now and will mean more as time goes on. Your thoughtful and kindly words of encouragement mean a lot to us. Thanks again for your thoughtfulness. Better yet, pray for us, and for God's will in all this.*

Here are some excerpts from Dan's journal:

16 July 1999. We had a great trip to England, returning home July 10 with lots of memories and pictures to share. On Tuesday our joy was changed to fear when Pat realized that the discomfort and swelling in her abdomen was not just constipation. But, God is good. He provided a clear path to evaluation and tests very swiftly to confirm our worst fears and an unexplained day off so I could be with her during the diagnostic tests. Pelvic ultrasound and CT scan show a large cystic and solid mass consistent with Ovarian Cancer. Blood test (CA125) is very high, suggesting the same.

We have gone from devastated to hopeful. We know both "too much" and "just enough." While it is quite scary, we know that this is the most curable adult female gynecological cancer. So, we are going to sit down, hold on to Jesus, and get ready for one hell of a ride.

22 July 1999. Pat had surgery this week to remove as much of the bulk of the tumor as possible. We must rely on the chemotherapy to get rid of the rest. That will start in a few weeks. The flood of prayers and concern has been a great encouragement. Many have called or emailed with their sentiments and spiritual wisdom. I requested an additional prayer that I would be able to keep a clear head so I could work effectively and not worry. Either I have been an oblivious fool or the Good Lord has provided me with His peace. I know deep in my heart that this is very serious and that some people (like my Aunt Ruth) die from this problem. For now we choose to not dwell on that but wait on the Lord for whatever is to come, one foot in front of the other. Thank you all so much for your emotional and prayer support.

26 July 1999. The euphoria of last week's progress and peace have begun to fade into the sobering reality of Pat's condition. People regularly die from this, and survival is not a guarantee. It leads to lots of existential questions. Not, "Why me?" But, "Why at all?' It must be for some good and for some permanent change in our lives and our relationships. Some literature suggests that pent up anger, resentment, or loneliness can lead to cancer, which is a sobering thought.

Pat really appreciates all the kind gestures on her behalf. It has buoyed her spirits during a very dark time. The cards, letters, flowers, balloons, calls, emails and visits have been remarkable. She is dearly loved by many.

Many people have been very encouraging to me too. I know there is a silver lining in this somewhere.

2 August 1999. I am frequently reminded of a poem we spotted near London in 1993. It was read by King George VI in his 1939 Christmas Radio message to the people of England just after declaring war on Germany. It is now displayed on a plaque at his grave in St. George's Chapel at Windsor Castle. It goes like this:

GOD KNOWS

by Minnie Louise Haskins

I said to the man who stood at the gate of the year,
Give me a light that I may tread safely into the unknown
(to us: will the chemo work? Will it be difficult? etc.)
And he replied: Go out into the darkness
And put your hand into the hand of GOD.
That shall be to you better than a light
And safer than a known way.

For someone in the business of being in control of people's lives, this is a hard test and a wonderful lesson to work through.

11 August 1999. We don't spend any time moping around and being sad. No time for that, and worry doesn't help. We cherish each day and smell the roses. God is trying to show us the way. This past Sunday one of the teenagers came back from a Mexico mission trip with some wisdom that has stuck with us. She learned a lot about trust from adversity on the trip. The analogy she came up with is that going through life and following God's plan is like driving home in the dark with headlights. You know you can make it home, but you are only allowed to see as far ahead as the headlight beam allows. Meanwhile, in an interview on TV, a 105-year-old lady pointed out, "Worry can kill you, you know!"

26 August 1999. Pat has had a really good week last week, walking more (brisk 60 minutes), some gardening, and able to do errands. Last Wednesday her scalp began to hurt like she had changed her part and the hair started to come out in increasing globs. By Friday night she asked me to get out the pet shears and finish it – better to have half-inch stubble than all that mess. Not traumatic, just "humbling." The wig and scarves and hats came out and most everyone was none the wiser.

I have resigned some of my administrative duties and begun reassessing how I spend my time and limited energy so I can devote more of it to nurturing Pat's health and state of mind. There are more simple household duties that Pat needs help with right now too. And I just like spending more time with her too. It is fun being "in love" again. Shucks. Why did it have to take cancer to show me this?

2 September 1999. We have good evidence that the chemo is working very well and Pat is right on schedule for a good response and a more favorable prognosis. Praise the Lord! And thank you for all those prayers that have helped. Besides the fact that Pat looks so good (even better with the wig on!), it is encouraging to see chemical evidence of progress. At times we get stuck in worry and fear as day-to-day decisions remind us of the specter of cancer. Your prayers and words of encouragement have been a big help to us. Hope is still alive and we are taking each day as a gift.

Speaking of hope, I wanted to share a brief poem that came on a card from one of Pat's friends. It is by Emily Dickinson:

Hope is the thing with feathers
That perches in the soul
And sings the tune without the words
And never stops at all.

21 September 1999. We are beginning to see a crack in the doorway to understanding that our journey is about a whole lot more than cancer. It is also about our relationships, our response to stress, our capacity to both live in the moment but to also appropriately plan for (not worry about) our future. I think we have turned a significant corner in hopefulness. We realize that Pat has a potentially fatal disease, but it isn't as scary as it was since she had good surgery, responds to chemotherapy, and her general health is good and handling the "trauma" fairly well. Oh, there is fatigue, mild imbalance, tingling in her fingers and toes, and I almost forgot loss of hair (the wig and scarves put that on the back shelf for us), and a significant drop in white count that could cause serious complications, BUT the reality is that she IS doing well right now and we think she has a fighting chance of being around for a while. So, we are trying to figure out what realistic plans we can make for the future and throw in a few dreams. It helps to enjoy our friendship RIGHT NOW.

25 September 1999. We had the blessing of meeting and making new friends while we were in Scotland, Al and Mary Beth DeHaven. They are Americans from Washington State who are working there in a missionary capacity. We have been blessed by their continued encouragement. They wrote to remind us that God tells us in the Scripture 366 times "Be not afraid," one for each day and an extra one for leap year! How we need that every day.

7 October 1999. I was trying to think last week, "What would I think if I had been given her prognosis? Try to walk in her moccasins." I honestly can't comprehend how it would feel. It isn't pretend. My clinically trained mind says it is always "somebody else." I am convinced there are several reasons why her 5-year survival is better than what the experts say it is. It is just hard right now to believe it with confidence. And I am not willing to give her up and call it "God's will." Not without a big fight and lots of pleading prayer, kicking and screaming!

19 October 1999. The end of the last chemo week was punctuated by some severe, brief episodes of nausea, which resolved. With all the medications she is taking for this and that, her ability to bounce back is really encouraging. We have been going to practice weekly (when we can) for a December performance of the Messiah. Pat has done it before, but this is my first. The music is really a blessing. We hope to be singing "The Hallelujah Chorus" with a new meaning this time.

The specter of death seems far off now, especially if I focus on Pat and not on statistics. All of us are mortal. Some of us just don't know it yet.

While Pat feels well enough to travel, she will be taking a one-week "rest" from her chemo schedule. The worry is, WHO WINS? Which will recover quicker from the chemo, the white cells or the tumor? Her oncologist said that by this time in her chemo, she would likely deserve this "rest." Pat's a little skeptical and requests that you specifically pray that this delay in the chemo sequence will not hinder her success in fighting this cancer. We want her to be well for this week with her family, but we want her immune system to recover, stay alert and active against this insidious tumor.

4 November 1999. We are hopeful that we were not tempting fate since in other types of therapy (radiation) you should not take "breaks" since the "opposing team is always on the field." Well, we thought it was a good idea to go and see Pat's father.

The trip to North Dakota went well—nice visit with Pat's father, Arthur. I didn't realize until I got away, how badly I needed the time off and the chance to have that prairie wind relieve my stress and clear my mind—and spend more time with Pat. It was a chance to read 2-3 books and get some insight and inspiration too.

28 November 1999. I am finally realizing that I have been going through "burnout" myself the past 6 months and was in denial about it. So, I am working on me and my attitude about it; and, learning more about how to trust in the Lord. I get anxious looking for ways to help Pat and wanting answers. Anxiety makes it worse. I am working on stress management with a new motivation—survival!

24 December 1999. The controversy has been whether to do "Second Look Surgery." Since this kind of cancer cannot be easily detected by clinical exam or CT Scan, Pat wants to know what is knowable. Findings of residual tumor result in a significantly different prognosis. One doesn't relish surgery for curiosity. As a compromise, it has been agreed that they can try a laparoscopic approach (Band-Aid, overnight stay). So, on Friday, January 7 she will have her laparoscopy, realizing there is risk of complications due to scar tissue resulting in possible need for a full open procedure and longer recovery, possible bowel injury too. Pat has been grateful for a 6-week period of recovery to get ready for this next step.

So, once again, we covet your prayers for a miracle of evidence for cure, of no surgical complications and a speedy recovery of body and spirit.

I will take most of next week off to rest, get a few things done, and just "be" before the next step in Pat's journey.

8 January 2000. No Laparoscopy. Open procedure was needed. The biopsies and cell washings are all negative, zero, none, zip! No evidence of any remaining cancer cells. Praise God!

In His kindness and undeserved mercy He has provided us the miracle we prayed for. I am listening to a recording from the Messiah: Worthy Is The Lamb, ***Blessing and honor and glory be unto Him, be unto Him, forever and ever, and ever, and ever, Amen, Amen, Amen, and Amen.*** (Pat isn't home so I can turn it up REAL LOUD and sing with it and REJOICE!) I'm not dancing, but almost. Those Baptist shoes are still nailed to the floor.

1 April 2000. We are very thankful for the miracle of her healing—something I have to admit at one time didn't seem possible. Some of you related examples of friends who did really well to give us hope. My cynicism didn't dare believe it was possible, so your encouragement helped. The prayers and love you all sent were very important. It has been interesting to notice that talk about cancer and illness no longer stirs the knot in my stomach or the pounding of my heart. We have been brought beside the still waters.

With Pat's recovery, I have had the energy to start looking ahead and contemplate options for my work situation, looking at solutions for my future there. There is a lot of change ahead that will suck a lot of energy from me. I am thankful that Pat is doing well, but I am very afraid of draining energy from my devotion to her. Life has hard choices. The real needs now are prayer for wisdom in the day-to-day when you are no longer in survival mode and risk missing the point in your most important relationships.

On Valentine's day, I had an image clear in my mind—God had taken me this past year to the edge of a cliff so I could look into the dark chasm that would have been life without Pat. I was terrified by that feeling of loss and loneliness and drawn to better understand how much I love Pat and value her companionship—in sickness and in health. My best buddy!

We have had the opportunity to see that others are going through crises, some with cancer and other life threatening illness. One friend has been cured by bone marrow transplant, another has recurrence of her ovarian cancer and is in hospice care, another desperately needs a lung transplant, another is starting chemotherapy for a Non-Hodgkin's Lymphoma, and another has recurrent ovarian cancer after a 5-year remission – one of my fears for Pat. Having been through our ordeal, we feel the privilege and desire to care about and pray for others. We understand, we have been there.

4 June 2000. The challenge is to stop and enjoy the present. I found myself just staring at Pat the other day at work and enjoying what I saw (Pat looking healthy, lively and beautiful). She thought I was spaced out. But in my defense, I was just practicing living in the moment. It wasn't that hard. I liked what I saw and it made me very happy.

We now turn to caring about others who need our love and prayers. We understand more now how important that is.

24 August 2000. The dream of a cure on first shot has been shattered. On to "Plan B," managing a "chronic disease." The emotions are mostly numbness and disappointment and the feeling of uncertainty about what the road ahead will look like.

We hope for a remission with each drug used that will buy time 'til the next is needed, sequentially, until they are able to find a new treatment that can actually cure. This will be a roller coaster. The goal is to maintain strength to fight while kicking butt on the cancer.

31 August 2000. "Been thinkin'" a lot, as you can imagine. Your e-mails and messages of love and support have been very meaningful to us: I was afraid some of the sympathy and tears would be depressing for Pat, but in Pat's words, they were "touching." Thank you so much for caring. Speechless was a common, authentic and loving response.

Dr. Newsom, bless his heart, was encouraging and hopeful there will be periods of remission and that quality of life may be there after each drug we try: treatment, remission, relapse, treatment, remission, relapse, etc., until a curative miracle drug comes along. We hope she can achieve a long enough response to see that day. She might even be able to keep her new curly hair this time. This time she again looks well and yet she has a tumor silently growing. Do you still see that healthy smiling face? That is the face of someone with Metastatic Ovarian Cancer.

I must remind myself that she still feels good and has good quality of life. I should not taint that with fear and sadness. Living in the present takes practice but adds joy and peace. I'm working on it. It encourages me to remain cheerful when I see Pat working at the office, strong and healthy, smiling and happy. I am astonished that somehow the word "cancer" doesn't seem to have the power to strike fear into my gut like it did even last week. The prayers must be helping, or maybe I'm just numb yet. But then, I don't have the feeling Pat has—"fullness in my stomach"—to remind me.

20 November 2000. Once again, Pat has asked me to send you an update regarding her ongoing concerns about her health and solicit your earnest prayers. In August her

CT scan showed convincing evidence of recurrent ovarian cancer.

The numerous examples of misfortune around us remind us that there are no guarantees and that continued good health is truly a gift. We come to this season of Thanksgiving with a thankful heart for the many blessings we have received. We also thank you for your faithfulness in remembering us. May God richly bless *you.*

18 December 2000. Pat's last CA 125 level on Friday again showed a slight increase from 93 to 117. We were disappointed that it is still rising, but we were glad that it was not even more.

Because of ongoing concerns about pain in her right side, she saw a consultant today who has scheduled her for a colonoscopy on Friday. We are hoping that he will only find scar tissue and not any evidence for tumor invading the bowel. If there are biopsies it will take a few days after to get the results. Merry Christmas? We hope so. Once again, we ask for your prayers, which you have so willingly offered.

27 January 2001. While Pat is generally feeling well and maintaining a normal activity level, we have decided that Pat should resume chemotherapy. The persisting pain in her side seems related to tumor nodules on the liver and diaphragm. It is more of an annoyance in severity and a reminder that something is not right. Even with effectively managing any bowel related symptoms, this discomfort continues.

31 March 2001. Pat resumed chemotherapy in January receiving a lighter dose of weekly Taxol, three weeks on and one week off. After six treatments she had a repeat CA-125 level (tumor marker level), and we were delighted that we saw a significant drop from over 200 to about 74. While this is still twice upper limit of normal, it is a significant improvement.

Life goes on and we have dreams. Pat has always wanted to see Ireland, so while our health permits, we are planning a trip to Ireland in June for 19 days. We're hoping this will be about the right time for a break in her chemo.

We're encouraged by the number of people who still indicate that they keep her in their prayers daily. How good it is to be part of the family of God, and to be the beneficiary of those kind souls who take the time to think of her. For those of you who feel the urging of the Spirit to do that, please don't stop.

10 May 2001. We wanted to let a few of you know about recent concerns. Because of some new symptoms, she saw her gynecologist who did a biopsy last Friday which revealed a nodule of cancer cells. The tumor is consistent with the cells she had from the ovarian cancer. It had been easier to accept a nebulous tumor hiding near the liver, but this one is within reach and more disturbing. It becomes harder to maintain our nonchalance about living with cancer.

12 May 2001. We got the pathology report on the biopsy on Tuesday. It was positive for recurrent

Adenocarcinoma consistent with ovarian cancer. She had a CT scan Thursday to look for other evidence of spread. The results were mixed. This is a chronic disease to be managed, not expecting a cure unless some miracle happens. Sheeesh!

Once again, we are reminded of the importance of smelling the roses and taking each day as it comes. We have never been on this road before. It is not a difficult one; it is just a road. Each day is more about living, and less about cancer in the challenge of "living with the cancer." Worry about the future has tried to creep in and has generated some healthy conversations that dispel anxiety. We are trying to balance enjoying the present while cautiously entertaining a few dreams.

18 May 2001. Pat had a minor procedure Wednesday…during the procedure they could look inside and clearly see evidence of tumor scattered on the pelvic sidewall. We'll have to rely on the chemotherapy and prayer to keep this in check. It is a blessing and a wonder that she feels this good. The concept of living each day one at a time is something that is getting less abstract.

27 May 2001. This has been an emotional roller coaster and at each step it requires that we process the challenge as we go on. There have been a lot of lessons to learn. One is that while we grieve over difficulties and fear, and then work through it, those around us go through this same process but at a different pace. So, while we move on and say we're doing fine, some of you are left behind in dismay and sadness, still processing your own grief. While it is difficult to know what to say during difficult times, we so much appreciate those who have given it their best shot. We have come to realize our problems may make others seem small or insignificant. In reality, our challenges do not diminish the hurts and needs of others. Actually, it's important for us to hear about other people's problems and concerns, taking the focus off our own.

I struggle with a weak faith that is easily overwhelmed by clinical realities and the pathology reports that tend to defeat hopefulness. Oh, I believe God can cure cancer, but do I have the courage to believe that He will? We so much appreciate the faithful prayers of many who do believe and continue to pray. This is encouraging to us.

9 June 2001. Pat had her last chemotherapy on May 31st and will take a break until we return from Ireland. We were disappointed to hear that her CA-125 tumor marker levels have continued to rise, suggesting that she is not responding to her current chemotherapy. When we return, the game plan will likely need to be changed, probably to something more toxic. We hope and pray that her holiday and immune system stimulator supplements will prove therapeutic. The difficult choices will involve selecting a new agent from either standard protocols or one of the numerous experimental protocols, too many choices.

Except for a little lack of stamina, Pat has been feeling quite well, able to work 2 days a week, do some walking to build her strength, and work in her garden. We really enjoy the many flowers in our yard that she has nurtured. While we are concerned about her long-term prognosis, we rejoice in the present. We must push aside dark thoughts about the future so they don't hinder reasonable hopes for ongoing treatment of this chronic disease. "Yesterday is history; tomorrow is a mystery; today is a gift; that's why it's called the present!"

8 July 2001. We safely returned from our wonderful trip to Ireland on June 29th. We had a good trip and made it back okay. It was really wonderful. The weather was Irish. We had a great time together and brought home lots of memories.

Before we left for Ireland, it was clear that Pat was failing to respond to her current chemotherapy with Taxol. The tumor cells seem to develop immunity, so you move on. On July 5th she started on her new regimen of Doxil by IV infusion every three weeks. Each drug has its own set of side effects so this will be a new experience. So far, so good, the more frequent problems are rashes on your hands and feet and more rare are cardiac damage. The fine print that comes with the drug is "too much information." The percentage of patients who respond is not encouraging, but better than no treatment. The oncologist is hopeful she will be one who responds favorably. We will follow the numbers and hang on to hope.

5 September 2001. I have been learning spiritual lessons about trusting God to work on things that are out of my control and not investing as much worry in the future, since now is pretty special. Honor and glory to Him for the peace He has given us.

22 September 2001. After the tragic events of the last few weeks, it was my intention to let you all know that we made it back home safely. We enjoyed a brief visit with family in Minneapolis, and fortunately had previously changed our plane reservation from Sept. 11 to Sept. 10th to fly on to North Dakota to visit with Pat's father. We were in innocent oblivion about world events until we received a phone call from our daughter, Annie, near Washington D.C. Considering the catastrophic events we were grateful to know that she was safe. She, with thousands of others, joined a huge traffic jam to evacuate Washington D.C. where she works at the British Embassy. We, like everyone, were stunned. We were thankful for our own safety, while transfixed by the media coverage, sad, and angry that the unbelievable had actually happened. I considered driving the three-day trip home if we couldn't fly, but we had no difficulty returning home on Monday the 17th. With all the security, there's no better time to fly.

25 November 2001. On this Thanksgiving holiday weekend, we pause to give thanks. With the crises and turmoil that has affected our nation and world, we are grateful for freedom and safety. We think of those who have been affected by tragedy, and those who currently place themselves in harm's way for the benefit of others and for our freedom.

On a personal level, we are thankful that Pat is doing as well as she is. It has been 28 months since initial diagnosis. We are grateful for each new day. Many of you have asked how she's doing. Actually, she is continuing to do quite well, with the exception of some mild fatigue, loss of stamina, and a nagging intermittent pain in her side. She has a monthly chemotherapy injection, which has been only a minor inconvenience. And she has not lost her hair, although the shedding of skin from her fingertips has almost eliminated her fingerprints. Weird. She keeps up with most home activities, and continues to work at least two days per week at the office. We are following her lab work closely, and have been disappointed a few times. Anyway, she looks real good, and I guess I'll go with that! I'm not prejudiced either. :-)

22 April 2002. Pat has developed new complications, which make her prognosis more uncertain. Her latest responses to chemotherapy have been disappointing and her side effects from it have made us both more discouraged. We still look for opportunities to have hope and rely more heavily on our faith and the support of friends and family.

From the beginning, I have struggled with a deep concern: Will I be able (now and later) to retain and maintain the capacity to have empathy for my patients with less than life-threatening issues while I am personally dealing with life-and-death matters? Will I be able to deal with someone's somatic complaints that arise in anxiety, or the pain from a stubbed toe, or somebody else's Chronic Fatigue Syndrome? Will I be able to function as a Wounded Healer?

It's easier said than done.

In fact, the week Pat had her first surgery, I "maxed out" emotionally with a patient who had a chronic condition involving moderate physical discomfort. She was difficult for me because she was very negative, always complaining, and very focused on herself and her aches and pains. I discharged her from my practice with a letter that I would not be able to care for her any longer. She was puzzled at first and expressed her annoyance to my nurse, but I think she knew it was more about my problems than hers. Her constant complaining, in light of symptoms so much less worrisome than Pat's, was the biggest reason I knew I couldn't continue to be objective in her care.

It is a valid issue for a physician or any other caregiver. I still struggle with it at times, but more often, as time has passed, I have been able to help others more because of my vulnerability. I think they are aware that I understand their struggles more than I could have ever understood them before.

> ***May God our Father and the Lord Jesus Christ give you his grace and peace. All praise to the God and Father of our Lord Jesus Christ. He is the source of every mercy and the God who comforts us. He comforts us in all our troubles so that we can comfort others. When others are troubled, we will be able to give them the same comfort God has given us*** (II Corinthians 1: 2-4).

SOURCES AND FURTHER READING

Andrescik, Robert, ***NewMan*** (July/August 2001, pgs. 25-28).

Bridges, Jerry, ***The Practice of Godliness*** (NavPress, Colorado Springs CO, 1983) pg. 124.

Calvin, John, ***Golden Booklet of the True Christian Life*** (Baker Book House, Grand Rapids MI, 1952) pgs. 15, 68-69.

Campbell, Tony, ***Together Journal.***

Chambers, Oswald, ***My Utmost For His Highest*** (Discovery House, Grand Rapids MI, 1992) July 16 reading.

Chambers, Oswald, ***Biblical Ethics, The Moral Foundations of Life, The Philosophy of Sin*** (Discovery House Publishers, Grand Rapids MI, 1998) pgs. 68, 328-332.

Chethik, Neil, ***Father Loss*** (Hyperion, New York NY, 2001) pg. 2,3,157,255,260,261.

Cohen, Richard, ***Coming Out Straight*** (Oakhill Press, Winchester, 2000) pg. 86.

Crabb, Larry, ***The Safest Place on Earth*** (Word, Nashville TN, 1999).

Curtis, Brent and John Eldridge, ***The Sacred Romance: Drawing Closer to the Heart of God*** (Thomas Nelson, Nashville TN, 1997) pg. 200.

Dalbey, Gordon, ***Sons of the Father*** (Tyndale House, Wheaton IL, 1996) pg. 28,36.

Dobson, Dr. James, ***When God Doesn't Make Sense*** (Tyndale House, Wheaton IL, 1993) pg. 41.

Dodd, Chip, ***The Voice of the Heart*** (Providence House, Franklin TN, 2001) pg.67, 81, 101.

Elias, Marilyn and Thoresen, Carl, ***USA Today*** (August 28, 2001) sub-title on the front page "Life: Forgiving Can Feel Good."

Green and McKnight, ***Dictionary of Jesus and the Gospels*** (InterVarsity Press, Downers Grove, IL, 1992) pg. 836, 838.

Hull, Bill, ***Jesus Christ Disciple-Maker*** (NavPress, Colorado Springs CO, 1984) pg. 166.

Jeffress, Robert, ***When Forgiveness Doesn't Make Sense*** (WaterBrook Press, Colorado Springs Co, 2000) pgs. 10-12,17, 56,82,127.

Johnson, Philip, ***Defeating Darwinism*** (InterVarsity Press, Downers Grove IL, 1997) pg.17.

Julian, Ron, ***Righteous Sinners: The Believers' Struggle with Faith, Grace, and Works*** (Nav Press, Colorado Springs, Co, 1998) pg.146.

Kane M.D., Jeff ***The Healing Companion*** (Harper, San Francisco CA, 2001) pgs.10,23,71.

Kataphygiotos, Kallistos, ***On Union with God and the Contemplative Life*** (pg 147:860A).

McClung Jr., Floyd, ***The Father Heart of God*** (Harvest House, Eugene OR 1985) pg.13-14, 40-41.

McIntosh, Pastor Mike, quoted by Jane Hansen, ***Fashioned for Intimacy*** (Regal Books, Ventura CA, 1979) pg. 26.

Medinger, Alan, ***Growth Into Manhood*** (WaterBrook Press, Colorado Springs CO, 2000) pgs.155, 171, 175, 224.

Men's Ministries, ***Honor Bound*** (Springfield, brochure/booklet).

Miller, Don & Lorna, ***Survivors*** (University of California Press, Berkeley and Los Angeles, CA – First paperback priority 1999, © 1993 by The Regents of the University of California) pgs. 157-163.

Moberly, Elizabeth, ***The Expository Times*** (June 1985) pg. 264.

Molitor, Brian D., ***A Boy's Passage*** (WaterBrook Press, Colorado Springs CO, 2001) pgs. 25, 187.

Nouwen, Henri J. M., ***The Wounded* Healer** (Image Books, Doubleday, New York NY, 1972) pg.27.

Piper, John, ***Desiring God*** (Multnomah, Sisters OR, 1996) pgs. 40,41.

P-Flag pamphlet, ***Why Ask Why? Addressing the Research on Homosexuality and Biology.***

Rainey, Dennis, ***The Tribute, What Every Parent Longs to Hear*** (Thomas Nelson, Nashville TN, 1994) pg.2, 3, 146-147.

Russell, George William, ***Book of Living Quotations in Pulpit Helps*** (September 2001) pg. 9.

Schmierer, Don, ***An Ounce Of Prevention*** (Promise Publishing, Santa Ana CA, 2002) pgs. 206-209.

Schmierer, Don, ***What's A Father To Do?*** (Promise Publishing, Santa Ana CA, 2000).

St. Dionysus the Areopagite, ***On The Divine Names*** (iv, 13, tr. Luibheid) pg 82.

Willard, Dallas, ***Divine Conspiracy*** (Exegesis of the Sermon on the Mount).

Wilmington, Dr. H.L., ***Williams Guide to the Bible*** (Tyndale House, Wheaton IL, 1981) pg. 306.

Yancey, Philip, ***Reaching for the Invisible God*** (Zondervan, Grand Rapids MI, 2000) pgs. 56, 57, 127.

Afterword

His Servants has created other materials to help parents, youth workers, ministry personnel and other concerned Christian adults deal with the problems of gender confusion in today's youth. We recommend the following:

An Ounce of Prevention

Preventing the Homosexual Condition In Today's Youth

by Don Schmierer with Lela Gilbert

In our complicated world, parents, young people, and youth leaders frequently face the subject of same-sex attractions. Author and seasoned counselor Don Schmierer provides a balanced perpective of this complex issue, discussing its various physical, emotional and spiritual aspects with wisdom and compassion.

"I must commend you on the sensitive, balanced, insightful treatment you gave this difficult subject. You managed to convey love and grace without dismissing homosexuality as a non-issue. You made yourself vulnerable and thus believable. You rightfully focused on building a healthy home environment and not on a sensational 'Ten Easy Steps...' approach."

Dr. Leroy Lawson, Pastor, President
Hope International University

What's A Father To Do?

Facing Parents' Toughest Questions

by Don Schmierer with Lela Gilbert

This concise and readable booklet speaks directly to dads about the problems that can arise with growing kids—problems like addictions, eating disorders, promiscuity, and same-sex attractions. One father writes, "I read with great interest your small booklet What's a Father to Do? Our second son had some traits that resembled 'Sean's.' You offered excellent advice in the booklet, which I followed. I must tell you that I experienced immediate results."

"Don Schmierer provides insightful and practical advice for parents struggling to build a positive home for their children. *What's a Father to Do* provides hope for those of us seeking to reconnect families across the nation."

Ken Canfield, Ph.D., President
National Center for Fathering

Celebrating God's Design

A Balanced and Biblical Perspective on Today's Toughest Youth Problems

by Don Schmierer with Lela Gilbert

In today's confusing world, kids have more questions than answers. *Celebrating God's Design* is a curriculum with a difference—allowing teenagers to talk, think and pray about such perplexing issues as gender, tolerance, sexuality, friendship, and family challenges. This one-of-a-kind, twelve-week youth curriculum features a stimulating video introduction to each session, included with the written material.

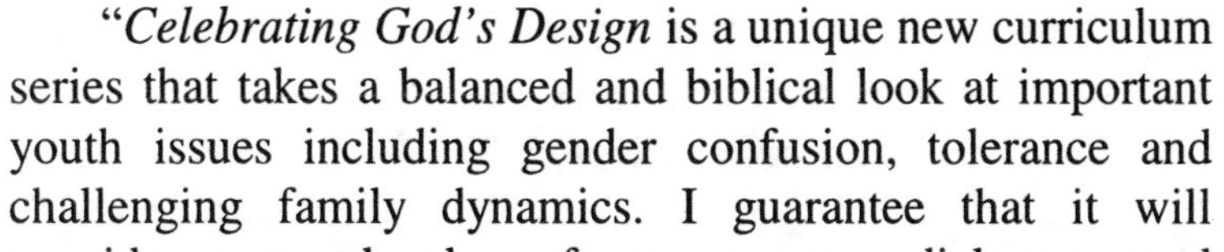

"*Celebrating God's Design* is a unique new curriculum series that takes a balanced and biblical look at important youth issues including gender confusion, tolerance and challenging family dynamics. I guarantee that it will provide new levels of awareness, dialogue and understanding among teens and those who work with them."

Jim Burns, Ph.D., President, YouthBuilders
(formerly National Institute of Youth Ministry)

Coming in 2003:

RX for Single Moms

Finding Help and Hope
When Dad's Not There

by Lela Gilbert with Don Schmierer

For further information, or to order any of these publications, contact:

His Servants
P. O. Box 765
Lockeford, CA 95237

http:// www.hisservants.net

http://www.youthbuilders.com